THE WRESTLER'S COOKBOOK

Recipes for High School Athletes

By Nicole Chambers

THE WRESTLER'S COOKBOOK

Recipes for High School Athletes

By Nicole Chambers

Published by CreateSpace, a DBA of On-Demand Publishing, LLC

ISBN-10: 146794985X
ISBN-13: 978-1467949859

Printed in the United States of America

For Shane

o o o o o

Table of Contents

Chapter 5

Chapter 6

Chapter 7

Chapter 8

Foreword

Blood. Sweat. Tears. Dedication. Commitment. Discipline. When you meet wrestlers, you quickly see that they proudly display these values and attributes. The many hours spent training in the gym might lead you to believe that simply "putting in the time" can lead to success. But if your son or daughter is a wrestler, you know that there is also time spent outside of the gym working to control weight. Finding nutritious, tasty and calorie conscious meals can be challenging. Poor nutritional intake leads to suboptimal performance, injury, and illness, thereby reducing the potential of your wrestler.

As a registered dietitian who specializes in Sports Nutrition, I work daily with athletes of all sports and ability levels, helping them to achieve peak performance by focusing on their nutritional intake. I specialize in wrestling nutrition because it is a sport that lacks sound, scientific nutritional research. This hinders attempts to make healthful eating recommendations for "making weight" during the season. Wrestling requires daily weight maintenance and current nutritional requirements and recommendations are frequently neglected. Ironically, of all the sports, success in wrestling is highly impacted by the athlete's daily nutrient intake. It is crucial that we expand the knowledge base regarding wrestling nutrition.

More information is needed about preparing healthy meals that will sustain our wrestlers throughout the long, wrestling season. Meals must fuel them with the proper blend of carbohydrates, proteins, fats (for strength and stamina) and electrolytes (to prevent dehydration), AND be appealing to the taste. Instead of zeroing in on calorie totals alone, parents and wrestlers should focus on eating delicious meals that are portioned appropriately and are nutritionally satisfying, in turn, helping the athletes to maintain their best power-to-weight ratio.

Nicole has gathered 60+ recipes that are easy, family-friendly, tasty, and most importantly, well balanced and nutrient dense. Recipe suggestions include a homemade sports drink, carbohydrate-rich granola bars for snacking on at matches, and an Asian salmon recipe rich in Omega-3 fatty acids which aid in reducing inflammation. You will find a variety of recipes for all meals and snacks designed to ensure that your wrestler is meeting his/her nutritional needs on competition day and every day in between.

Move past the "water and toast diet" and expand your wrestler's horizons with the wholesome, nutrient-packed meals in The Wrestler's Cookbook.

Kim Tirapelle, MS, RD, CSSD is the Sports Dietitian for TERRIO Physical Therapy & Fitness in Fresno, CA. She is also the Team Dietitian for Fresno State Athletics, and the Clovis (CA) High School Wrestling team, which captured it's state-record ninth team title in 2011 and has finished in the top five in the state for each of the last five years.

o o o o o

Preface

As the mother of a high school wrestler, I was frustrated with my son not wanting to eat as a way of maintaining his weight. As it turned out, other wrestlers' parents were having the same problem!

So, I spent my son's sophomore year assembling a cookbook from recipes collected over time. My main goal was getting the kids to eat, rather than taking the weight loss approach. These recipes focus on good nutrition, high protein, low fat content and vitamins. They are easy to make, tasty and family friendly! In addition, you will find that each recipe includes per serving nutritional data such as calorie information and protein, carbohydrate, sodium and sugar values using USDA calculations.

In the beginning pages, you will find other helpful information. You can determine how many calories your wrestler should consume daily by using a chart based on the Katch-McArdle Formula. Also listed, in chart form, are common foods that are good sources of proteins, carbohydrates and antioxidants. You will also find several pages of wrestler 'factoids' peppered throughout the book.

Having done the research, I find that my initial instincts were right, and yours are, too - a healthy wrestler performs better. Wrestling is a grueling sport and the kids work hard to compete during a long season. I hope that this cookbook will be helpful to you and your wrestler!

Nicole Chambers

Chapter 1
Information

Stick to the following basics as the core of your menu system:

Proteins are vital to good wrestling performance. They assist in muscle recovery after vigorous exercise. Protein also helps build muscle while training and lifting.

Complex Carbohydrates (not simple carbs like sugar or starch) such as grains are great for wrestlers. They are digested more slowly, providing fuel over longer periods of time.

Low-Fat foods provide necessary fuel while helping to keep daily fat intake at the recommended level of 60 to 65 grams. Stay away from saturated fats!

Fluids are essential, period. Long workouts and tough, demanding matches speed up dehydration. Stay hydrated with water. Serve a glass of low-fat milk with dinner, and check out the recipe for homemade sports drink for when your wrestler needs to replenish electrolytes lost through perspiration.

Antioxidants and Vitamin C are found in lots of fruits, veggies and spices. Both are very helpful in helping the immune system fight off bacterial and skin infections that are often transmitted between wrestlers as a result of close contact.

Sodium requirements for an athlete are greater than the average person's upper limit of 2,300 mg /day. The American College of Sports Medicine recommends consuming drinks that contain 500/700 mg of sodium per hour while under intense training to maintain electrolyte balance.

1

Daily Caloric Intake Chart
values based on Katch–McArdle formula

% Body Fat:

	7%	8%	9%	10%	11%	12%	15%	20%	25%
100	1283	1273	1263	1254	1244	1234	1205	1155	1106
110	1374	1364	1353	1342	1331	1320	1288	1234	1180
120	1466	1454	1442	1430	1419	1407	1371	1313	1254
130	1557	1544	1531	1519	1506	1493	1455	1391	1327
140	1648	1635	1621	1607	1593	1580	1538	1470	1401
150	1740	1725	1710	1695	1681	1666	1622	1548	1475
160	1831	1815	1800	1784	1768	1752	1705	1627	1548
170	1922	1906	1889	1872	1855	1839	1789	1705	1622
180	2014	1996	1978	1961	1943	1925	1872	1784	1695
190	2105	2086	2068	2049	2030	2012	1956	1862	1769
200	2196	2177	2157	2137	2118	2098	2039	1941	1843
210	2287	2267	2246	2226	2205	2184	2123	2019	1916
220	2379	2357	2336	2314	2292	2271	2206	2098	1990
230	2470	2448	2425	2402	2380	2357	2289	2177	2064
240	2561	2538	2514	2491	2467	2444	2373	2255	2137
250	2653	2628	2604	2579	2555	2530	2456	2334	2211

Weight: (row labels)

Note: lose weight by reducing intake by 500 calories / day
gain weight by adding extra 500 calories / day

Food Reference Chart

Food Type	Complex Carbs	Protein	Anti oxidant
Bread; bagel, multi grain		x	
Bread; bagel, whole wheat		x	
Fruit, berries, all			x
Fruit; apples			x
Fruit; cherries		x	
Fruit; grapefruit, pink	x		x
Fruit; grapes, red			x
Fruit; kiwi			x
Fruit; lemons		x	
Fruit; mangoes			x
Fruit; Melon, cantaloupe		x	x
Fruit; melon, honeydew			x
Fruit; nectarines			x
Fruit; oranges	x		x
Fruit; papaya			x
Fruit; peaches			x
Fruit; pears		x	
Fruit; plums			x
Fruit; prunes			x
Fruit; pumpkin, canned		x	x
Fruit; raisins			x
Fruit; raspberries		x	
Fruit; strawberries			x
Fruit; tangerines			x
Fruit; watermelon		x	x
Grain; barley	x		
Grain; buckwheat	x		

Food Reference Chart – cont.

Food Type	Complex Carbs	Protein	Anti oxidant
Grain; bulgar		x	
Grain; millet	x		
Grain; oat bran		x	
Grain; oats	x		
Grain; quinoa	x	x	
Grain; rice, brown	x	x	
Grain; rice, wild		x	
Grain; rye	x		
Grain; shredded wheat		x	
Grain; wheat	x		
Legume; beans, black		x	
Legume; beans, garbanzo		x	
Legume; beans, kidney	x	x	
Legume; beans, lima	x	x	
Legume; beans, navy	x	x	
Legume; beans, pinto	x	x	
Legume; beans, white	x	x	
Legume; garbanzo	x		
Legume; lentil	x	x	
Legume; peas, black-eyed	x	x	
Legume; peas, split	x		
Meat; buffalo		x	
Meat; chicken, white		x	
Meat; beef		x	
Meat; lamb		x	
Meat; mackerel		x	
Meat; pork tenderloin		x	

Food Reference Chart – cont.

Food Type	Complex Carbs	Protein	Anti oxidant
Meat; salmon		x	
Meat; sirloin steak		x	
Meat; tuna		x	
Meat; turkey, white		x	
Nuts; all		x	x
Pasta; whole wheat		x	
Seeds; popcorn	x		
Seeds; pumpkin		x	
Seeds; sesame		x	
Seeds; sunflower		x	x
Veg; sweet potato	x		
Veg; alfalfa sprouts			x
Veg; apricots			x
Veg; artichoke		x	
Veg; asparagus	x		x
Veg; beans, green	x		
Veg; beets			x
Veg; broccoli	x	x	x
Veg; brussels sprouts		x	x
Veg; carrots			x
Veg; cassava	x		
Veg; cauliflower	x		x
Veg; chard			x
Veg; corn	x		x
Veg; dark green leafy veg	x		
Veg; eggplant			x
Veg; greens, collard			x

Food Reference Chart – cont.

Food Type	Complex Carbs	Protein	Anti oxidant
Veg; greens, mustard			x
Veg; greens, turnip			x
Veg; kale		x	x
Veg; leeks		x	
Veg; mushrooms	x		
Veg; onions	x		x
Veg; parsnip	x		
Veg; peas, green	x	x	
Veg; peppers, all	x		x
Veg; potato, sweet			x
Veg; potato, white	x	x	
Veg; rutabaga	x		
Veg; snow peas			x
Veg; soybeans	x		
Veg; spinach			x
Veg; squash	x		x
Veg; tomato, cooked	x		
Veg; tomato, fresh			x
Veg; turnip		x	x
Veg; yam	x		

FACTOIDS

✦ *The most important nutrient for any athlete is water.*

✦ *To grow naturally and increase strength, wrestlers need the same nutrients as other teenagers, but need more calories to meet the demands of daily training.*

✦ *Fasting causes the body to use muscle proteins for energy even if fat is available.*

✦ *Hydrate with water, gatorade, fruit juices and skim milk.*

✦ *Losing weight rapidly results in a loss of both muscle tissue and water.*

✦ *Sports drinks help replenish the body's supply of electrolytes, which are lost through perspiration.*

✦ *Practicing good nutrition and proper weight control methods is vital to achieving peak physical performance.*

✦ *The more you worry about your weight, the less you concentrate on your wrestling.*

✦ *Not all fat on your body can be considered "excess" fat. A certain amount of fat is essential for use as energy, to act as a shock absorber for your internal organs, to insulate your body from the cold, and to store certain nutrients.*

✦ *If you are thirsty, you're already dehydrated.*

✦ *Seven percent body fat is considered the lowest healthy level of fat content for teenage males.*

✦ *Most wrestlers perform very well at a higher percentage of body fat.*

✦ *A wrestler's caloric intake should not fall below 1,700-2,000 calories per day.*

Chapter 2
Breakfast

HEARTY OATMEAL

2 servings

Hearty Oatmeal recipe
1 ½ cups **water**
2 dashes **sea salt**
¼ cup **brown sugar**
1 tablespoon **raisins**
1 tablespoon **cranberries, dried**
2 tablespoons **pecans, chopped**
1 dash **cinnamon, ground**
1 cup **oats, rolled**

NUTRITION FACTS	
Servings:	2
Amount Per Serving	
Calories:	310
Total Fat:	6.87 g
Cholesterol:	0 mg
Sodium:	154 mg
Total Carbs:	58.95 g
Dietary Fiber:	4.73 g
Sugars:	30.73 g
Protein:	6.12 g

1. Combine all ingredients except oats and bring just to boil.

2. Add oats, stir well and reduce to low boil and cook for 5 minutes. Serve with lowfat milk if desired.

Source: Nicole Chambers

HOT BANANA NUT CEREAL

Add raisins or dried cranberries for extra flavor!

2 servings

Banana Nut Cereal recipe
¾ cup **water**
¾ cup **milk, 99% fat free**
3 tablespoons **quinoa**
2 tablespoons **walnuts, chopped**
2 tablespoon **brown sugar**
2 dashes **sea salt**
3 dashes **cinnamon, ground**
½ teaspoon **vanilla extract**
1 medium **banana, mashed**
½ cup **oats, rolled**

NUTRITION FACTS	
Servings:	2
Amount Per Serving	
Calories:	449
Total Fat:	7.85 g
Cholesterol:	4 mg
Sodium:	195 mg
Total Carbs:	97.14 g
Dietary Fiber:	31.58 g
Sugars:	27.35 g
Protein:	11.83 g

1. Stir the water, milk, and quinoa together in a saucepan; bring to a gentle boil. Reduce heat to low. Stir in walnuts, brown sugar, salt, cinnamon and vanilla. Simmer 5 minutes, or until the quinoa begins to soften.

2. Add banana and rolled oats. Cook, stirring frequently over low heat for 2 to 5 minutes or until mixture thickens. Remove from heat and serve.

Source: adapted from HomesKillet's Good-Morning Banana Nut Cereal

BANANA WHOLE WHEAT WAFFLES

4 servings

Banana Whole Wheat Waffles recipe
¾ cup **all-purpose flour**
¾ cup **whole wheat flour**
2 ½ teaspoons **baking powder**
½ teaspoon **sea salt**
1 pinch **nutmeg, ground**
1 pinch **cinnamon, ground**
1 large **egg**
1 cup **milk, 99% fat free**
½ teaspoon **vanilla extract**
2 tablespoons **orange juice**
1 tablespoon **honey**
2 **banana, ripe, mashed**

NUTRITION FACTS	
Servings:	4
Amount Per Serving	
Calories:	327
Total Fat:	2.39
Cholesterol:	49 mg
Sodium:	640 mg
Total Carbs:	56.87 g
Dietary Fiber:	4.67 g
Sugars:	15.64 g
Protein:	9.74 g

1. Preheat waffle iron. In a medium mixing bowl, whisk together flours, baking powder, salt, nutmeg and cinnamon.

2. Beat egg in separate medium to large bowl. Add milk, vanilla, orange juice, honey and banana and blend until smooth. Add flour mixture in 3 parts, stirring after each addition.

3. Spray preheated waffle iron with cooking spray. Pour waffle batter onto the hot waffle iron. Cook until golden brown. Serve hot.

Source: Nicole Chambers

WHOLE WHEAT BLUEBERRY PANCAKES

6 servings

Whole Wheat Blueberry Pancakes recipe

2 ½ cups **whole wheat flour**

1 tablespoon **baking powder**

2 **egg**

2 cups **milk, 99% fat free**

1 teaspoon **vanilla extract**

1 teaspoon **sea salt**

2 tablespoon **natural sugar**

1 cup **blueberries**

NUTRITION FACTS	
Servings:	6
Amount Per Serving	
Calories:	258
Total Fat:	3.04 g
Cholesterol:	58 mg
Sodium:	688 mg
Total Carbs:	48.64 g
Dietary Fiber:	5.95 g
Sugars:	11.20 g
Protein:	11.37 g

1. Sift together flour and baking powder, set aside. Beat together the egg, milk, vanilla, salt and sugar. Add flour mixture and stir until moistened, adding more milk if necessary. Gently fold in blueberries.

2. Preheat a heavy-bottomed skillet or griddle. Spray with cooking spray. Pour enough batter onto hot griddle to make 6" pancakes. Cook until bubbly and underside is golden. Turning only once, continue cooking until golden brown.

Source: adapted from Brossette Lewis' Whole Wheat Blueberry Pancakes

Chapter 3

Breads & Muffins

NO KNEAD WHOLE WHEAT ROLLS

12 servings

No Knead Whole Wheat Rolls recipe
1 ¼ cups **whole wheat flour**
1 cup **all-purpose flour**
2 tablespoons **natural sugar**
½ teaspoon **sea salt**
1 package **yeast, active dry**
1 cup **milk, 99% fat free**
3 tablespoons **butter, melted**
1 medium **egg, lightly beaten**

NUTRITION FACTS	
Servings:	12
Amount Per Serving	
Calories:	129
Total Fat:	3.52 g
Cholesterol:	22 mg
Sodium:	136 mg
Total Carbs:	20.33 g
Dietary Fiber:	1.78 g
Sugars:	3.24 g
Protein:	4.15 g

1. Mix together flours, sugar, salt and yeast in a medium bowl. In large bowl, whisk milk, melted butter and egg until well blended. Add flour mixture to egg mixture and blend well. Cover bowl and place in oven with light on until doubled in size, about 1 hour.

2. Spray muffin tin with cooking spray. Stir dough to de-gas and spoon into muffin tin. Preheat oven to 400°F. Let rise until the dough crests top of muffin tin. Bake rolls in preheated oven for 15 to 20 minutes or until golden brown.

Source: Marilyn Tellefsen

HEALTHY GRAIN BREAD

Have a bread machine? Follow steps as outlined in 7 Grain Bread.

12 servings

Healthy Grain Bread recipe
2 teaspoons **yeast, active dry**
⅛ teaspoon **natural sugar**
3 tablespoons **warm water**
½ cup **warm water**
2 teaspoons **honey**
2 teaspoons **molasses**
1 tablespoon **vegetable oil**
1 small **egg**
1 teaspoon **lemon juice**
1 ⅛ cups **whole wheat flour**
2 teaspoons **flax seed**
2 teaspoons **wheat bran**
1 tablespoon **sunflower seeds**
½ teaspoon **sea salt**
¾ cup **bread flour**

NUTRITION FACTS	
Servings:	12
Amount Per Serving	
Calories:	97
Total Fat:	2.13 g
Cholesterol:	6 mg
Sodium:	100 mg
Total Carbs:	16.90 g
Dietary Fiber:	1.87 g
Sugars:	1.76 g
Protein:	3.24 g

1. In small bowl, dissolve 1/8t yeast and sugar in 3T warm water. In large bowl, mix remaining 1/2 cup warm water, honey, molasses, oil, egg and lemon juice. Mix well. Add yeast mixture and stir.

2. In medium bowl, combine whole wheat flour, flax, wheat bran, sunflower seeds and salt. Stir into mixture from previous step until well combined.

3. Let rise in covered bowl for 20 minutes.

4. Stir in bread flour until dough pulls away from the sides of the bowl. Knead on floured surface for 10 to 15 minutes or until dough is smooth and elastic. Put into a greased bowl. Cover and let rise until doubled, about 45 minutes.

5. Preheat oven to 375 F.

6. Punch down and shape into ball. Cover and let rest for 20 minutes.

7. Form into loaf and place on greased cookie sheet. Cover and let rise until doubled. Bake in preheated oven for 25–35 minutes or until internal temperature reaches 200 degrees.

Source: adapted from Dee's Health Bread

WHOLE WHEAT BREAD

12 servings

Whole Wheat Bread recipe
1 cup warm water, 110 degrees
2 teaspoons **yeast, active dry**
2 tablespoons **honey**
1 ⅔ cups **bread flour**
1 tablespoon **butter, melted**
1 ½ tablespoons **honey**
1 teaspoon **sea salt**
1 ¼ cups **whole wheat flour**
1 cup **whole wheat flour**

NUTRITION FACTS	
Servings:	12
Amount Per Serving	
Calories:	174
Total Fat:	1.56 g
Cholesterol:	2 mg
Sodium:	203 mg
Total Carbs:	35.32 g
Dietary Fiber:	3.06 g
Sugars:	5.18 g
Protein:	5.55 g

1. In a large bowl, mix warm water, yeast, and 2T honey. Add bread flour and stir until well blended. Let sit for 30 minutes.

2. Add melted butter, 1 1/2T honey, and salt and stir. Mix in whole wheat flour and blend well. Flour a flat surface and knead with leftover whole wheat flour until mildly sticky, use more flour if necessary. Place in lightly greased bowl, turning once to coat the surface of the dough. Cover and let rise in a warm place until doubled, about 45 minutes.

3. Preheat oven to 350 F.

4. Punch down and place in greased 9 x 5 inch loaf pans, and allow to rise until dough has topped the pans by one inch.

5. Bake in preheated oven for 25 to 30 minutes, until golden brown, or internal temperature reaches 200 degrees.

Source: adapted from Nita Crabb's Simple Whole Wheat Bread

7 GRAIN BREAD

Can also be made in a bread machine using standard procedure.

12 servings

7 Grain Bread recipe

⅔ cup **warm water, 110 degrees**

½ teaspoon **yeast, active dry**

1 small **egg**

4 ½ tsp **milk, dry powder, non-fat**

1 tablespoon **vegetable oil**

1 tablespoon **honey**

½ cup **whole wheat flour**

1 ¼ cups **bread flour**

1 teaspoon **sea salt**

⅓ cup **cereal, 7 grain**

1 ½ teaspoons **yeast, active dry**

1 teaspoon **corn meal**

NUTRITION FACTS	
Servings:	12
Amount Per Serving	
Calories:	96
Total Fat:	1.55 g
Cholesterol:	6 mg
Sodium:	206 mg
Total Carbs:	17.23 g
Dietary Fiber:	1.17 g
Sugars:	2.12 g
Protein:	3.30 g

1. Place warm water and 1/2 teaspoon yeast in the bread machine pan. Let sit for 5 minutes.

2. Beat egg in separate bowl. Mix in powdered milk, oil and honey. Add to bread machine pan.

3. In medium bowl, combine flours, salt, cereal and yeast with whisk. Spoon into bread machine pan.

4. Select 1 hour cycle and run machine until kneading stops. Remove from bread machine and place dough into bowl greased lightly with cooking spray. Cover with damp towel and let rise 45 minutes, or until double in size.

5. Preheat oven to 450 degrees.

6. Remove dough from bowl and place on floured surface. Knead 1 to 2 minutes. Flatten into 10" to 12" circle. Roll tightly into loaf and place on cookie sheet sprinkled with corn meal. Slice top of loaf with sharp knife and let rise for 15 minutes.

7. Place loaf in preheated oven, reduce heat to 425 and bake until crust is browned and internal temperature reaches 200 degrees. Let cool for 15 minutes before slicing.

Source: adapted from Pat's Seven Grain Bread

ZUCCHINI BREAD

2 slices per serving, 1/2" thick.

12 servings

Zucchini Bread recipe
1 ½ cups **all-purpose flour**
½ teaspoon **sea salt**
½ teaspoon **baking soda**
½ teaspoon **baking powder**
1 teaspoon **cinnamon, ground**
2 small **eggs**
¼ cup **vegetable oil**
¼ cup **applesauce, unsweetened**
1 teaspoon **vanilla extract**
½ cup **natural sugar**
½ cup **brown sugar**
1 cup **zucchini, grated**
½ cup **walnuts, chopped**

NUTRITION FACTS	
Servings:	12
Amount Per Serving	
Calories:	310
Total Fat:	11.70 g
Cholesterol:	20 mg
Sodium:	268 mg
Total Carbs:	46.79 g
Dietary Fiber:	1.53 g
Sugars:	27.49 g
Protein:	4.44 g

1. Grease and flour an 8 x 4 inch loaf pan. Preheat oven to 325 degrees F.

2. Gently whisk flour, salt, baking soda, baking powder and cinnamon together in a bowl. In separate large bowl, beat eggs, oil, applesauce, vanilla, and sugars together. Add sifted ingredients to the creamed mixture, and beat well. Stir in zucchini and nuts until well combined. Pour batter into prepared pans.

3. Bake in preheated oven for 40 to 60 minutes, or until tester inserted in the center comes out clean. Cool in pan on rack for 30 minutes before slicing.

Source: adapted from V Monte's Mom's Zucchini Bread

BANANA NUT MUFFINS

For less calories and fat, substitute equal amount of unsweetened applesauce. Nutritional information calculated using vegetable oil.

12 servings

Banana Nut Muffins recipe
¾ cup **all-purpose flour**
¾ cup **whole wheat flour**
1 cup **oats, rolled**
¼ cup **natural sugar**
¼ cup **brown sugar, packed**
2 teaspoons **baking powder**
1 teaspoon **baking soda**
½ teaspoon **sea salt**
1 medium **egg**
¾ cup **milk, 99% fat free**
⅓ cup **vegetable oil**
½ teaspoon **vanilla extract**
1 cup **banana, mashed**
¼ cup **walnuts, chopped**

NUTRITION FACTS	
Servings:	12
Amount Per Serving	
Calories:	210
Total Fat:	8.34 g
Cholesterol:	14 mg
Sodium:	296 mg
Total Carbs:	30.25 g
Dietary Fiber:	2.29 g
Sugars:	12.01 g
Protein:	4.26 g

1. Preheat oven to 350 F.

2. In medium bowl, combine flours, oats, sugars, baking powder, baking soda, and salt.

3. In a large bowl, beat the egg lightly. Stir in the milk, oil (or applesauce), and vanilla. Add the mashed banana, and combine thoroughly. Gradually add flour mixture and stir until just combined. Fold in walnuts.

4. Line a 12-cup muffin tin with paper baking cups, and divide batter between them. Bake in preheated oven for 18 to 20 minutes, or until golden brown.

Source: adapted from Karen Resciniti's Banana Oat Muffins

MORNING GLORY MUFFINS

12 servings

Morning Glory Muffins recipe
1 ½ cups **all-purpose flour**
½ cup **whole wheat flour**
1 ¼ cup **natural sugar**
1 tablespoon **cinnamon, ground**
2 teaspoons **baking powder**
½ teaspoon **baking soda**
½ teaspoon **sea salt**
1 medium **egg**
2 medium **egg whites**
1 cup **applesauce, unsweetened**
1 tablespoon **vanilla extract**
2 cups **carrots, shredded**
1 medium **apple, peeled, cored & chopped**
1 cup **raisins**
½ cup **walnuts, chopped**

NUTRITION FACTS	
Servings:	12
Amount Per Serving	
Calories:	261
Total Fat:	3.62 g
Cholesterol:	13 mg
Sodium:	259 mg
Total Carbs:	54.13 g
Dietary Fiber:	3.26 g
Sugars:	33.00 g
Protein:	4.73 g

1. Preheat oven to 350 degrees F. Lightly grease muffin tin or use paper liners.

2. In a medium bowl, combine flours, sugar, cinnamon, baking powder, baking soda and salt.

3. In a large bowl, whisk together egg, egg whites, applesauce and vanilla. Stir in carrots, apple and raisins. Gradually add flour mixture and stir until just moistened. Fold in walnuts.

4. Spoon the batter into the prepared muffin cups, distributing equally.

5. Bake in preheated oven for about 20 minutes, or until the tops are golden and spring back when lightly pressed.

Source: adapted from Jaclyn's Morning Glory Muffins

BLUEBERRY BRAN MUFFINS

12 servings

Blueberry Bran Muffins recipe
1 ½ cups **wheat bran**
1 cup **milk, 99% fat free**
1 medium **egg, separated**
½ cup **applesauce, unsweetened**
⅔ cup **brown sugar**
1 teaspoon **vanilla extract**
½ cup **all-purpose flour**
½ cup **whole wheat flour**
1 teaspoon **baking soda**
1 teaspoon **baking powder**
½ teaspoon **cinnamon, ground**
½ teaspoon **sea salt**
1 cup **blueberries**

NUTRITION FACTS	
Servings:	12
Amount Per Serving	
Calories:	124
Total Fat:	.97 g
Cholesterol:	16 mg
Sodium:	261 mg
Total Carbs:	28.59 g
Dietary Fiber:	4.24 g
Sugars:	15.49 g
Protein:	3.65 g

1. Preheat oven to 375 degrees F. Grease muffin tin or use paper liners. Mix together wheat bran and milk. Let stand for 10 minutes.

26

2. Separate egg yolk from white and set each aside. In a large bowl, mix together egg yolk, applesauce, brown sugar, and vanilla. Mix in bran mixture.

3. Gently whisk together flours, baking soda, baking powder, cinnamon and salt. Stir into bran mixture until just blended. Fold in blueberries.

4. Beat egg white until fluffy and fold into mixture.

5. Scoop into muffin cups.

6. Bake in preheated oven for 15 to 20 minutes, or until tops spring back when lightly tapped.

Source: adapted from 3LionsCubs' Low-Fat Blueberry Bran Muffins

Chapter 4
Soups

LAMB & BARLEY SOUP

8 servings

Lamb & Barley Soup recipe
1 lb. **lamb, stew meat**
½ medium **onion, chopped**
4 cups **tomatoes, stewed with oregano & garlic**
6 cups **water**
4 teaspoons **beef bouillon powder**
1 tablespoon **natural sugar**
4 medium **carrots, chopped**
3 medium **celery stalks, chopped**
¾ cup **barley**
¾ teaspoon **rosemary, dried**
¾ teaspoon **thyme, dried**
¼ teaspoon **black pepper, ground**
⅛ teaspoon **cayenne pepper**

NUTRITION FACTS	
Servings:	8
Amount Per Serving	
Calories:	273
Total Fat:	12.56 g
Cholesterol:	41 mg
Sodium:	818 mg
Total Carbs:	21.32 g
Dietary Fiber:	4.17 g
Sugars:	5.43 g
Protein:	16.85 g

Saute lamb and onion in large soup pot over medium heat until browned. Drain. Add tomatoes, water, bouillon powder and sugar. Stir in carrots, celery, and barley. Add rosemary, thyme and black and cayenne peppers. Simmer covered for 1 hour over medium low heat.

Source: Nicole Chambers

SWEET POTATO, CARROT, APPLE, AND RED LENTIL SOUP

6 servings

Sweet Potato, Carrot, Apple, and Red Lentil Soup recipe
¼ cup **olive oil**
2 cups **sweet potatoes, peeled and chopped**
3 **carrots, peeled and chopped**
1 **apple, peeled, cored and chopped**
1 **onion, chopped**
½ cup **red lentils**
¼ teaspoon **ginger powder**
½ teaspoon **black pepper, ground**
1 teaspoon **sea salt**
½ teaspoon **cumin, ground**
½ teaspoon **chili powder**
½ teaspoon **paprika**
4 cups **vegetable broth**

NUTRITION FACTS	
Servings:	6
Amount Per Serving	
Calories:	230
Total Fat:	9.10 g
Cholesterol:	0 mg
Sodium:	1069 mg
Total Carbs:	34.93 g
Dietary Fiber:	6.32 g
Sugars:	14.03 g
Protein:	3.68 g

1. Warm the olive oil in a large pot over medium-high heat. Place the chopped sweet potatoes, carrots, apple, and onion in the pot. Cook until the onions are translucent, about 10 minutes.

2. Stir in lentils, ginger, pepper, salt, cumin, chili powder, paprika, and vegetable broth into the pot with the apple and vegetable mixture. Bring the soup to a boil over high heat. Reduce to medium–low, cover, and simmer until the lentils and vegetables are soft, about 30 minutes.

3. Working in batches, pour the soup into a blender, no more than halfway full. Carefully start the blender, using a few quick pulses to get the soup moving before leaving it on to puree. Puree in batches until smooth and pour into large saucepan.

4. Simmer over medium heat for 10 minutes. Thin soup with water to desired consistency.

Source: adapted from Allrecipes, Zhidaoma's Sweet Potato, Carrot, Apple and Red Lentil Soup

SPLIT PEA AND HAM SOUP

8 servings

Split Pea and Ham Soup recipe
7 cups **cold water**
1 ½ teaspoons **chicken bouillon**
2 ¼ cups **split peas, dried**
2 lbs. **ham steak, cooked, chopped**
2 medium **onion, sweet, thinly sliced**
½ teaspoon **sea salt**
¼ teaspoon **black pepper, ground**
2 dashes **cayenne pepper**
2 teaspoons **garlic powder**
⅛ teaspoon **sage, ground**
⅛ teaspoon **marjoram, dried**
1 cup **cooking sherry**
3 medium **celery stalks, chopped**
3 medium **carrots, chopped**
2 medium **potatoes, chopped**

NUTRITION FACTS	
Servings:	8
Amount Per Serving	
Calories:	374
Total Fat:	4.22 g
Cholesterol:	61 mg
Sodium:	1692 mg
Total Carbs:	51.23 g
Dietary Fiber:	21.70 g
Sugars:	12.29 g
Protein:	47.22 g

1. Combine water and bouillon in stockpot. Once boiling, add peas. Simmer gently for 2 minutes. Remove from heat and set aside for 1 hour.

2. Add ham, onion, salt, peppers, garlic powder, sage and marjoram. Add sherry and stir well. Cover, bring to boil and then simmer for 1 1/2 hours, stirring occasionally.

3. Place chopped celery, carrots and potatoes into food processor. Run food processor until finely chopped. Add to soup along with peas and cook on low while covered, for one hour. Stir frequently and add water as necessary.

Source: Nicole Chambers

LOWFAT ASIAN STYLE SOUP

Alternatively, you can substitute cooked chicken for shrimp.

8 servings

Lowfat Asian Style Soup recipe

½ tablespoon **olive oil**

2 teaspoons **ginger powder**

2 tablespoons **garlic**

¼ cup **cornstarch**

4 cups **chicken broth, fat free**

½ cup **mushrooms, canned, drained**

½ cup **bamboo shoots, drained**

¼ cup **soy sauce, light**

2 tablespoons **rice wine vinegar**

1 ½ teaspoons **natural sugar**

½ teaspoon **crushed red pepper**

2 pkg **vegetables, stir-fry vegetables, frozen 10 oz pkg**

1 lb. **shrimp, precooked, peeled and deveined shrimp**

2 tablespoons **cilantro, fresh**

½ pkg **spinach, frozen chopped, (10 ounce) package, thawed and drained**

NUTRITION FACTS	
Servings:	8
Amount Per Serving	
Calories:	161
Total Fat:	1.50 g
Cholesterol:	119 mg
Sodium:	1355 mg
Total Carbs:	18.33 g
Dietary Fiber:	3.95 g
Sugars:	1.65 g
Protein:	17.48 g

1. In large stock pot, saute' ginger and garlic in olive oil for 3 minutes. Lower heat. Add cornstarch and stir well. Slowly stir in chicken broth.

2. Add mushrooms, bamboo shoots, soy sauce, vinegar, sugar, and crushed red pepper and bring to a boil. Lower heat to medium high and stir until soup thickens.

3. Stir in mixed vegetables, shrimp (or chicken) and cilantro. Simmer about 10 minutes. Stir in spinach and continue simmering for 2 minutes. Serve hot.

Source: adapted from Lil Hen's Miracle Soup

TORTILLA CHICKEN & VEGETABLE SOUP

4 servings

Tortilla Chicken & Vegetable Soup recipe
1 tablespoon **olive oil**
½ cup **water**
4 ounces **tomato sauce**
1 cup **vegetable broth**
1 ½ cups **chicken broth, fat free**
1 teaspoon **garlic powder**
2 tablespoons **chili powder**
1 teaspoon **cumin, ground**
½ teaspoon **sea salt**
2 cups **pinto beans, canned, drained**
1 cup **tomatoes, stewed w/ oregano & garlic**
1 cup **corn, frozen**
1 tablespoon **cilantro, fresh**
½ cup **chicken breast, cooked, cubed**
2 oz. **tortilla chips, lowfat, crushed**

NUTRITION FACTS	
Servings:	4
Amount Per Serving	
Calories:	298
Total Fat:	6.86 g
Cholesterol:	14 mg
Sodium:	1629 mg
Total Carbs:	45.16 g
Dietary Fiber:	9.36 g
Sugars:	3.35 g
Protein:	15.94 g

1. In large pot, bring to simmer olive oil, water, tomato sauce and broths. Add garlic powder, chile powder, cumin and salt. Bring just to boil then reduce heat to low.

2. Add beans, tomatoes, corn, cilantro and chicken. Simmer for 15 minutes.

3. Top with crushed tortilla chips and serve.

Source: Nicole Chambers

Chapter 5
Salads

ASIAN CUCUMBER SALAD

4 servings

Asian Cucumber Salad recipe
2 tablespoons **sesame oil**
2 teaspoons **dill, dried**
½ cup **rice wine vinegar**
¼ cup **mirin (Japanese rice wine)**
1 teaspoon **sesame seeds, white**
1 teaspoon **sesame seeds, black**
2 medium **cucumbers, sliced**
1 dash **cayenne pepper, optional**

NUTRITION FACTS	
Servings:	4
Amount Per Serving	
Calories:	95
Total Fat:	7.25 g
Cholesterol:	--
Sodium:	95 mg
Total Carbs:	4.01 g
Dietary Fiber:	.96 g
Sugars:	1.74 g
Protein:	1.03 g

1. Stir together sesame oil, dill, rice vinegar, mirin, and sesame seeds in a glass or plastic bowl. Warm in microwave for 1 minute on power level 5. Add cucumber, and toss until well coated. Spice with cayenne pepper to your liking.

2. Cover, and refrigerate for 2 hours.

Source: unknown

BROCCOLI SALAD

6 servings

Broccoli Salad recipe
8 slices **bacon, cooked, crumbled**
3 **broccoli crowns, bite size pieces**
¼ cup **onion, red, chopped**
½ cup **grapes, red, seedless, halved**
3 tablespoons **white wine vinegar**
2 tablespoons **natural sugar**
1 cup **mayonnaise, light**
1 cup **sunflower seeds**

NUTRITION FACTS	
Servings:	6
Amount Per Serving	
Calories:	601
Total Fat:	45.79 g
Cholesterol:	11 mg
Sodium:	550 mg
Total Carbs:	32.22 g
Dietary Fiber:	10.70 g
Sugars:	11.71 g
Protein:	16.62 g

1. Cook bacon over medium high heat until evenly brown. Drain, crumble and set aside.

2. In a medium bowl, combine the broccoli, onion and grapes. In a small bowl, whisk together the vinegar, sugar and mayonnaise. Pour over broccoli mixture, and toss until well mixed. Refrigerate for at least two hours.

3. Before serving, toss salad with crumbled bacon and sunflower seeds.

Source: adapted from Allrecipes, J John's Alyson's Broccoli Salad

THREE BEAN SALAD

10 servings

Three Bean Salad recipe
2 cups **black beans, canned, drained**
2 cups **kidney beans, canned, drained**
2 cups **cannellini beans, canned, drained**
½ cup **bell pepper, green, chopped**
½ cup **bell pepper, red, chopped**
1 ¼ cups **corn, frozen, thawed, drained**
¾ cup **onion, red, chopped**
½ cup **olive oil**
½ cup **red wine vinegar**
2 tablespoons **lime juice, fresh
                or bottled**
1 tablespoon **lemon juice**
4 teaspoons **natural sugar**
1 tablespoon **sea salt**
1 clove **garlic, crushed**
¼ cup **cilantro, fresh, chopped**
½ tablespoon **cumin, ground**
½ tablespoon **black pepper, ground**
1 dash **hot pepper sauce**
½ teaspoon **chili powder**

NUTRITION FACTS	
Servings:	10
Amount Per Serving	
Calories:	262
Total Fat:	11.7 g
Cholesterol:	0 mg
Sodium:	1088 mg
Total Carbs:	30.99 g
Dietary Fiber:	9.47 g
Sugars:	5.09 g
Protein:	9.33 g

1. In a large bowl, combine drained beans, bell peppers, corn, and red onion.

2. In a small bowl, whisk together olive oil, red wine vinegar, lime juice, lemon juice, sugar, salt, garlic, cilantro, cumin, and black pepper. Season to taste with hot sauce and chili powder. Pour olive oil dressing over vegetables; mix well. Serve warm or cold.

Source: adapted from Karen Castle's Mexican Bean Salad

PERFECT SPINACH SALAD

Nutritional info was calculated using blue cheese. Leaving blue cheese out reduces calories by 40 per serving.

8 servings

Perfect Spinach Salad recipe
2 tablespoons **sesame seeds, white**
2 tablespoons **pecans, chopped**
½ cup **natural sugar**
2 teaspoons **onion**
¼ cup **white wine vinegar**
¼ cup **cider vinegar**
½ cup **olive oil**
1 tablespoon **olive oil**
¾ cup **pine nuts, blanched**
        and slivered
1 lb. **spinach, fresh, rinsed**
        and torn
1 cup **cranberries, dried**
½ cup **mandarin oranges, canned**
½ cup **blue cheese, crumbled**

NUTRITION FACTS	
Servings:	8
Amount Per Serving	
Calories:	391
Total Fat:	26.19 g
Cholesterol:	6 mg
Sodium:	165 mg
Total Carbs:	32.45 g
Dietary Fiber:	3.55 g
Sugars:	24.25 g
Protein:	6.08 g

1. Combine sesame seeds, pecans, sugar, onion, vinegars, and olive oil in medium sized bowl and mix well. Set aside.

2. In a medium saucepan, heat remaining olive oil over medium heat. Saute' pine nuts in oil until lightly toasted. Remove from heat, and let cool.

3. In a large salad bowl, combine the spinach, cranberries, mandarin oranges and toasted pine nuts. Toss gently.

4. Toss spinach with dressing just before serving. Sprinkle with crumbled blue cheese if desired.

Source: Nicole Chambers

CORNUCOPIA SALAD

8 servings

Cornucopia Salad recipe
Dressing:
2 tablespoons **red wine vinegar**
2 teaspoons **natural sugar**
salt and pepper to taste
¼ cup **olive oil**
¼ cup **almonds, sliced**
1 tablespoon **natural sugar**
1 head **lettuce, red leaf, torn**
3 medium **green onions, chopped**
1 medium **apple, cored and chopped**
1 medium **avocado, peeled, pitted, chopped**
½ cup **cranberries, dried**
¼ cup **blue cheese, crumbled**

NUTRITION FACTS	
Servings:	8
Amount Per Serving	
Calories:	187
Total Fat:	12.62 g
Cholesterol:	3 mg
Sodium:	71 mg
Total Carbs:	16.87 g
Dietary Fiber:	3.63 g
Sugars:	11.04 g
Protein:	2.71 g

1. In small bowl, whisk together red wine vinegar, 2t sugar, salt and pepper and olive oil. Set aside.

2. Place the almonds and 1 tablespoon of sugar in a small skillet over medium–low heat, and cook and stir until the sugar melts and the almonds brown, watching carefully to avoid burning. Remove from heat and allow to cool.

3. In a large salad bowl, mix the lettuce, green onions, apple, avocado, dried cranberries, blue cheese, and cooked almonds. Pour the dressing over the salad, gently toss and serve.

Source: Allrecipes, Christine's Cornucopia Salad

44

FRUITY ROMAINE SALAD

Also great with poppyseed dressing!

6 servings

Fruity Romaine Salad recipe
1 head **lettuce, romaine, torn**
½ cup **swiss cheese, lowfat,
      shredded**
1 cup **cashews**
¼ cup **cranberries, dried**
1 medium **apple, peeled, diced**
½ cup **mandarin oranges, drained**
1 medium **pear, peeled, sliced**
¼ cup **dressing, vinegrette**

NUTRITION FACTS	
Servings:	6
Amount Per Serving	
Calories:	226
Total Fat:	10.94 g
Cholesterol:	3 mg
Sodium:	144 mg
Total Carbs:	27.41 g
Dietary Fiber:	5.22 g
Sugars:	14.71 g
Protein:	7.76 g

In a large serving bowl, toss together the romaine
lettuce, shredded Swiss cheese, cashews, cranberries,
apple, mandarin oranges and pear. Pour your favorite
vinegarette dressing over salad just before serving, and
toss to coat.

Source: Nicole Chambers

Chapter 6

Main Dishes

REALLY TENDER PORK ROAST

The meat of this roast is so tender and falls right off the bone!

8 servings

Really Tender Pork Roast recipe
6 lb. pork roast, boston butt
2 cloves **garlic, quartered (long)**
2 tablespoons **olive oil**
2 teaspoon **garlic powder**
1 teaspoon **sea salt**
1 teaspoon **black pepper, ground**

NUTRITION FACTS	
Servings:	8
Amount Per Serving	
Calories:	821
Total Fat:	46.91 g
Cholesterol:	289 mg
Sodium:	590 mg
Total Carbs:	0.71 g
Dietary Fiber:	0.12 g
Sugars:	0.02 g
Protein:	82.50 g

1. Preheat oven to 400 degrees F. Using a sharp paring knife, make 6 randomly spaced 1" deep slits in fleshy part of roast. Poke one sliver of garlic deep into each hole. Place roast fat side up in rack. Mix garlic powder, salt and pepper together and pat down on top of roast.

2. Place roast on middle rack in oven. Reduce heat to 250 degrees F. Cook 6 – 8 hours, basting at least twice until internal temperature reaches 160 degrees. Slice and serve.

Source: Nicole Chambers

GRILLED PORK TENDERLOIN IN GREEK MARINADE

If you can't grill, this dish may be cooked in a 350 oven for 45 minutes.

6 servings

Grilled Pork Tenderloin in Greek Marinade recipe

2 lbs. **pork tenderloin**

1 ½ cups **lime juice, fresh or bottled**

¾ cup **olive oil**

6 cloves **garlic, chopped**

2 teaspoons **sea salt**

6 tablespoons **oregano, dried**

NUTRITION FACTS	
Servings:	6
Amount Per Serving	
Calories:	445
Total Fat:	31.14 g
Cholesterol:	98 mg
Sodium:	865 mg
Total Carbs:	7.17 g
Dietary Fiber:	1.58 g
Sugars:	1.00 g
Protein:	31.84 g

1. Cut tenderloin into 2" strips.

2. Place lime juice, olive oil, garlic, salt, and oregano in a large resealable plastic bag. Shake sealed bag until ingredients are well mixed. Place tenderloin strips into bag, seal, and turn to coat. Marinate in the refrigerator for 2 to 5 hours.

3. Preheat grill for medium heat.

4. Lightly oil the grill grate. Grill tenderloins, basting with marinade, for 15 to 20 minutes or until juices run clear.

Source: adapted from Dave Nash's Grecian Pork Tenderloin

LEMON HERB PORK CHOPS ON THE GRILL

6 servings

Lemon Herb Pork Chops recipe
¼ cup **lemon juice**
2 tablespoons **olive oil**
4 cloves **garlic, minced**
1 teaspoon **sea salt**
¼ teaspoon **oregano, dried**
¼ teaspoon **black pepper, ground**
6 pork loin chops, boneless

NUTRITION FACTS	
Servings:	6
Amount Per Serving	
Calories:	239
Total Fat:	10.40 g
Cholesterol:	75 mg
Sodium:	746 mg
Total Carbs:	1.41 g
Dietary Fiber:	0.12 g
Sugars:	0.27 g
Protein:	33.91 g

1. In a large resealable bag, combine lemon juice, oil, garlic, salt, oregano, and pepper. Place chops in bag, seal, and refrigerate 2 hours or overnight. Turn bag frequently to distribute marinade.

2. Preheat grill to medium high heat. Remove chops from bag, and transfer remaining marinade to a saucepan. Bring marinade to a boil, remove from heat, and set aside.

3. Grill pork chops for 5 to 10 minutes per side, or until juices run clear, basting frequently with boiled marinade.

Source: Allrecipes, Doreen Buch's Grilled Lemon Herb Pork Chops

BAKED PORK TENDERLOIN

6 servings

Baked Pork Tenderloin recipe
¼ cup **olive oil**
½ cup **white wine**
½ teaspoon **black pepper, ground**
1 tablespoon **garlic powder**
2 lbs. **pork tenderloin**
1 cup **red wine**
½ medium **onion, thinly sliced**
1 cup **mushrooms, fresh, sliced**
½ teaspoon **garlic powder**
¼ teaspoon **sea salt**
¼ teaspoon **black pepper, ground**
1 pkg **brown gravy mix, (.75 ounce) packet dry**

NUTRITION FACTS	
Servings:	6
Amount Per Serving	
Calories:	643
Total Fat:	22.46 g
Cholesterol:	107 mg
Sodium:	4101 mg
Total Carbs:	50.63 g
Dietary Fiber:	2.96 g
Sugars:	8.33 g
Protein:	38.56 g

1. Combine olive oil, white wine, 1/2t pepper and 1T garlic powder. Marinate tenderloin in mixture for 1 hour.

2. Combine red wine, onion and mushrooms together in medium bowl. Set aside. In small dish, mix garlic powder, salt and pepper together. Set aside.

3. Preheat oven to 325 degrees F.

4. Place pork and marinade in a 9x13 dish. Cover with wine, onion and mushroom mixture. Sprinkle with garlic/salt/pepper mixture.

5. Cover and bake for 1 hour. Remove meat from baking dish and keep warm.

6. Whisk gravy mix into pan juices over low heat. Serve over sliced pork.

Source: Nicole Chambers

BEEF CHILI

10 servings

Beef Chili recipe
2 lbs. **ground beef, 85% lean**
3 cups **chili beans, canned, drained**
1 cup **chili beans, spicy, canned**
6 cups **tomatoes, canned, diced with juice**
1 can **tomato paste**
1 medium **onion, sweet, chopped**
3 medium **celery stalks, chopped**
1 medium **bell pepper, green, seeded and chopped**
1 medium **bell pepper, red, seeded and chopped**
2 small **chile pepper, poblano, seeded and chopped**
2 slices **bacon, cooked, crumbled**
4 cubes **beef bouillon powder**
¼ cup **chili powder**
½ cup **beer, non-alcoholic**
1 tablespoon **worcestershire sauce**
1 tablespoon **garlic powder**
1 tablespoon **oregano, dried**
2 teaspoons **cumin, ground**
2 teaspoons **hot pepper sauce**
1 teaspoon **basil, dried**
1 teaspoon **sea salt**
1 teaspoon **black pepper, ground**
1 teaspoon **cayenne pepper**
1 teaspoon **paprika**
1 teaspoon **natural sugar**
½ cup **sour cream, light**
1 cup **cheddar cheese, lowfat, shredded**

NUTRITION FACTS	
Servings:	10
Amount Per Serving	
Calories:	408
Total Fat:	14.74 g
Cholesterol:	66 mg
Sodium:	1383 mg
Total Carbs:	36.01 g
Dietary Fiber:	9.94 g
Sugars:	12.63 g
Protein:	29.54 g

1. In large stock pot, over medium-high heat, cook ground beef until evenly browned. Drain off excess fat.

2. Add chili beans, spicy chili beans, diced tomatoes and tomato paste. Stir until combined. Add the onion, celery, green and red bell peppers, chile pepper, bacon bits, bouillon powder, chili powder and beer. Stir and simmer for 15 minutes. Add worcestershire sauce, garlic, oregano, cumin, hot pepper sauce, basil, salt, pepper, cayenne, paprika, and sugar. Stir, cover and simmer over low heat for two to three hours, stirring occasionally.

3. Top with a spoonful of light sour cream and shredded cheddar cheese.

Source: adapted from Allrecipes, MightyPerdue22's Boilermaker Tailgate Chili

REMPEL FAMILY MEATLOAF

There is a 2 piece, self-draining, meatloaf pan available that allows the fat to pass down into the bottom pan as the meatloaf cooks.

6 servings

Rempel Family Meatloaf recipe
1 ½ lbs. **ground beef, 85% lean**
24 **buttery round crackers, crushed**
¾ cup **cheddar cheese, lowfat**
    & shredded
1 packet **onion soup mix**
2 medium **eggs, beaten**
¼ cup **ketchup**
2 tablespoons **steak sauce**

NUTRITION FACTS	
Servings:	6
Amount Per Serving	
Calories:	386
Total Fat:	19.82 g
Cholesterol:	134 mg
Sodium:	987 mg
Total Carbs:	16.61 g
Dietary Fiber:	0.76 g
Sugars:	4.35 g
Protein:	27.98 g

1. Preheat oven to 350 degrees F.

2. Mix the ground beef, crushed crackers, cheddar cheese, and onion soup mix in a large bowl until well combined. Whisk the eggs, ketchup, and steak sauce in a separate bowl until smooth. Add the egg mixture to the meat until evenly combined. Press into a 9x5 inch loaf pan.

3. Bake in preheated oven until the meatloaf reaches 160 degrees F and is no longer pink in the center, 45 to 60 minutes.

Source: Allrecipes, Connie Levesque

POT ROAST

8 servings

Pot Roast recipe
½ pkg **brown gravy mix**
2 tablespoons **water**
1 pkg **onion soup mix**
1 can **low sodium cream of mushroom soup**
2 cloves **garlic, chopped**
1 can **cola carbonated beverage**
4 lbs. **beef, sirloin roast**
1 lb. **carrots, baby**
1 medium **onion, quartered**
3 **celery stalks, cut into 2" lengths**

NUTRITION FACTS	
Servings:	8
Amount Per Serving	
Calories:	600
Total Fat:	21.18 g
Cholesterol:	181 mg
Sodium:	2123 mg
Total Carbs:	34.48 g
Dietary Fiber:	3.50 g
Sugars:	11.19 g
Protein:	64.69 g

1. In a small bowl, combine the brown gravy mix and water, mixing into a smooth paste. Add onion soup mix, cream of mushroom soup, garlic and cola-flavored carbonated beverage. Stir well. Pour 1/3 in the bottom of slow cooker.

2. Place meat in slow cooker. Arrange carrots, onion, celery and garlic around roast. Pour remaining mixture from step one over roast.

3. Cook on High for 3.5 to 4 hours, OR on Low (preferred) setting for 8 to 9 hours.

Source: adapted from Sher Garfield's Cola Pot Roast

SIRLOIN TIP ROAST

6 servings

Sirloin Tip Roast recipe
1 ¼ tablespoons **paprika**
2 teaspoons **sea salt**
1 teaspoon **garlic powder**
½ teaspoon **black pepper, ground**
½ teaspoon **onion powder**
½ teaspoon **cayenne pepper**
½ teaspoon **oregano, dried**
½ teaspoon **thyme, dried**
2 tablespoons **olive oil**
3 lbs. **beef, sirloin roast**

NUTRITION FACTS	
Servings:	6
Amount Per Serving	
Calories:	459
Total Fat:	21.77 g
Cholesterol:	176 mg
Sodium:	900 mg
Total Carbs:	1.62 g
Dietary Fiber:	0.73 g
Sugars:	0.19 g
Protein:	61.03 g

1. Preheat oven to 350 degrees F. Line a baking sheet with aluminum foil.

2. In small bowl, mix together paprika, salt, garlic powder, black pepper, onion powder, cayenne pepper, oregano, and thyme. Stir in the olive oil, and allow the mixture to sit about 15 minutes.

3. Place roast on the prepared baking sheet, and cover on all sides with the spice mixture. Roast uncovered for 1 hour in preheated oven, or to minimum internal temperature of 145 degrees F. Let sit 10 minutes before slicing.

Source: Allrecipes, Joel's Herb Rubbed Sirloin Tip Roast

BRAISED CHICKEN

6 servings

Braised Chicken recipe

3 lbs. **chicken breast**

2 dashes **black pepper, ground**

1 teaspoon **garlic powder**

2 tablespoons **olive oil**

1 medium **onion, thinly sliced**

¼ cup **balsamic vinegar**

¼ cup **chicken broth, fat free**

2 cups **tomatoes, canned, diced with juice**

1 teaspoon **basil, dried**

1 teaspoon **oregano, dried**

1 teaspoon **rosemary, dried**

½ teaspoon **thyme, dried**

NUTRITION FACTS	
Servings:	6
Amount Per Serving	
Calories:	331
Total Fat:	8.43 g
Cholesterol:	145 mg
Sodium:	419 mg
Total Carbs:	7.46 g
Dietary Fiber:	1.39 g
Sugars:	4.31 g
Protein:	49.22 g

1. Season chicken breasts with ground black pepper and garlic powder. Heat olive oil in a medium skillet, and brown the seasoned chicken breasts and onion.

2. In small bowl, stir together balsamic vinegar, chicken broth and tomatoes. Pour mixture over chicken. Season with basil, oregano, rosemary and thyme. Cover and simmer until chicken is no longer pink and the juices run clear, about 15 minutes.

Source: adapted from Allrecipes, MoonAndBack's Braised Balsamic Chicken

CHICKEN BARBEQUE

6 servings

Chicken Barbeque recipe
6 chicken breast, boneless halves
1 ½ cups **barbecue sauce**
⅓ cup **olive oil**
2 tablespoons **balsamic vinegar**
2 tablespoons **brown sugar**
1 tablespoon **honey**
1 tablespoon **steak sauce**
1 tablespoon **worcestershire sauce**

NUTRITION FACTS	
Servings:	6
Amount Per Serving	
Calories:	410
Total Fat:	4.37 g
Cholesterol:	151 mg
Sodium:	1078 mg
Total Carbs:	34.53 g
Dietary Fiber:	0.49 g
Sugars:	27.65 g
Protein:	50.29 g

1. In small bowl, mix together barbecue sauce, olive oil, vinegar, brown sugar, honey, steak sauce and Worcestershire sauce. Pour 1/2 mixture into slow cooker.

2. Place chicken atop sauce in cooker and cover with remaining sauce.

3. Cover, and cook 3 to 4 hours on High or 6 to 8 hours on Low (or until chicken falls apart). Serve on whole wheat buns or over brown rice.

Source: Nicole Chambers

LEMON CHICKEN WITH ANGEL HAIR

No grill? Cover and bake in 350 oven for 1 hour.

8 servings

Lemon Chicken with Angel Hair recipe
½ cup **olive oil**
3 teaspoons **garlic**
1 teaspoon **rosemary, dried**
1 teaspoon **thyme, dried**
¾ teaspoon **oregano, dried**
⅜ cup **lemon juice**
8 **chicken breast, cut into strips**
1 lb. **whole wheat angel hair pasta**
2 tablespoons **olive oil**

NUTRITION FACTS	
Servings:	8
Amount Per Serving	
Calories:	392
Total Fat:	17.26 g
Cholesterol:	151 mg
Sodium:	276 mg
Total Carbs:	1.33 g
Dietary Fiber:	0.22 g
Sugars:	0.29 g
Protein:	50.24 g

1. In a glass dish, mix the olive oil, garlic, rosemary, thyme, oregano, and lemon juice. Pour mixture into sturdy zipper bag. Place chicken pieces in the bag and remove as much air as possible. Marinate in the refrigerator overnight.

2. Fill large spaghetti pot halfway with water. Bring to boil. Add angel hair to boiling water and cook on medium high for 3 minutes. Remove from heat and drain. Add 2T olive oil and distribute evenly. Keep warm.

3. Cook chicken on the hot grill, baste with marinade while cooking. Grill appx. 10 minutes per side, or until juices run clear. Serve over whole wheat angel hair pasta.

Source: Nicole Chambers

SPANISH CHICKEN AND RICE CASSEROLE

8 servings

Spanish Chicken and Rice Casserole recipe

1 ⅓ cups **brown rice**

2 ⅔ cups **water**

1 teaspoon **chicken bouillon**

8 **chicken breast**

1 can **cream of chicken soup
Healthy Request**

½ cup **water**

1 medium **onion, chopped**

1 ½ cups **salsa**

4 tablespoons **sour cream, light**

3 cups **cheddar cheese, lowfat
& shredded**

NUTRITION FACTS	
Servings:	8
Amount Per Serving	
Calories:	491
Total Fat:	8.12 g
Cholesterol:	161 mg
Sodium:	947 mg
Total Carbs:	31.91 g
Dietary Fiber:	2.21 g
Sugars:	3.24 g
Protein:	64.21 g

1. Combine rice, water and chicken bouillon in a saucepan. Bring to a boil. Reduce heat, cover and simmer for 20 minutes.

2. Place chicken breast halves into a large saucepan filled with water. Bring to a boil, reduce heat and simmer for 15 minutes, or until done. Drain. Add cool water to stop chicken from cooking. Drain and cut chicken into bite size pieces. Set aside.

3. Preheat oven to 350 degrees F.

4. In a separate bowl, mix together cream of chicken soup, water, onion, salsa and sour cream.

5. In 9x13 baking dish, layer half of the rice, half of the chicken, half of the soup/salsa mixture, and half of the cheese in prepared dish. Repeat, ending with cheese.

6. Bake in preheated oven for about 40 minutes, or until bubbly.

Source: Nicole Chambers

CHICKEN CHILI

This entree can also be made in the slow cooker by combining all ingredients and cooking on low for 8 hours.

8 servings

NUTRITION FACTS	
Servings:	8
Amount Per Serving	
Calories:	303
Total Fat:	5.61 g
Cholesterol:	29 mg
Sodium:	960 mg
Total Carbs:	41.07 g
Dietary Fiber:	5.66 g
Sugars:	8.29 g
Protein:	19.39 g

Chicken Chili recipe
1 cup **onion, red, chopped**
2 tablespoons **olive oil**
2 cloves **garlic, minced**
2 cups **chicken broth, fat free**
2 cups **salsa verde, 18 oz jar**
2 cups **tomatoes, canned and
         diced with juice**
1 cup **chile pepper, poblano, chopped**
½ teaspoon **oregano, dried**
½ teaspoon **coriander, ground**
½ teaspoon **cumin, ground**
1 ½ cups **corn, canned, drained**
2 cups **chicken breast, cooked, diced**
2 cups **white beans, canned**
salt and pepper to taste
½ cup **tortilla chips, lowfat, crushed**

1. Set aside 1/8 cup chopped onion for garnish.

2. Heat oil, and cook remaining onion and garlic until soft.

3. Stir in broth, salsa verde, tomatoes, chilies, and spices. Bring to a boil and simmer for 10 minutes.

4. Add corn, chicken, and beans; simmer 5 minutes. Season with salt and pepper to taste. Garnish with red onion and crushed tortilla chips.

Source: adapted from Thea's White Bean Chicken Chili

LAMB STEW

10 servings

Lamb Stew recipe
12 slices **bacon, raw, diced**
6 lbs. **lamb, stew meat, cut into 2 inch pieces**
½ teaspoon **sea salt**
½ teaspoon **black pepper, ground**
½ cup **all-purpose flour**
4 ½ cups **water**
2 teaspoons **natural sugar**
2 teaspoons **beef bouillon powder**
1 packet **onion soup mix**
1 teaspoon **thyme, dried**
2 **bay leaves**
¾ cup **cooking sherry**
3 cloves **garlic, minced**
2 medium **onion, sweet, quartered**
4 cups **carrots, baby**
4 medium **potatoes, cut into 2 in pieces**

NUTRITION FACTS	
Servings:	10
Amount Per Serving	
Calories:	575
Total Fat:	16.00 g
Cholesterol:	187 mg
Sodium:	1192 mg
Total Carbs:	35.38 g
Dietary Fiber:	3.64 g
Sugars:	7.68 g
Protein:	62.81 g

1. Place bacon in a large, deep skillet. Cook over medium high heat until evenly brown. Remove bacon from pan and crumble. Set aside.

2. Put lamb, salt, pepper, and flour in large mixing bowl. Toss to coat meat evenly. Brown meat in frying pan with bacon fat.

3. Place meat into slow cooker. Add the water, sugar, bouillon, onion soup mix, thyme, bay leaves and cooking sherry to the slow cooker. Stir. Add bacon, garlic and onion. Cook on high for 2 hours.

4. Add carrots and potatoes. Continue cooking in slow cooker on high for 2 more hours.

Source: Nicole Chambers

WHOLE WHEAT PIZZA

This recipe will help satisfy the pizza urge.

6 servings

Whole Wheat Pizza recipe
¾ cup **warm water**
1 tablespoon **olive oil**
½ teaspoon **honey**
1 teaspoon **yeast, bread machine**
1 cup **whole wheat flour**
1 cup **flour**
1 ¼ teaspoons **yeast, bread machine**
1 teaspoon **sea salt**
2 oz. **tomato sauce**
8 oz. **mozzarella, non-fat, shredded**
½ medium **bell pepper, green, chopped**
½ medium **onion, chopped**

NUTRITION FACTS	
Servings:	6
Amount Per Serving	
Calories:	231
Total Fat:	2.96 g
Cholesterol:	6 mg
Sodium:	719 mg
Total Carbs:	34.64 g
Dietary Fiber:	4.23 g
Sugars:	2.31 g
Protein:	17.59 g

1. Pour warm water into bread machine. Add olive oil, honey and 1 tsp yeast. Let sit for 5 minutes.

2. Stir flours, yeast, and salt together.

3. Preheat oven to 450.

4. Add flour mixture to water mixture in bread machine. Set on 1 hour cycle. When kneading has stopped, unplug machine and place dough in lightly greased bowl. Cover and let sit for 30 minutes.

5. Remove dough from bowl and knead briefly. Press into 14" deep pizza pan and bake for 3 minutes.

6. Remove from oven. Top evenly with tomato sauce. Sprinkle shredded cheese atop sauce. Add peppers and onions.

7. Bake on low rack in oven, checking periodically, for 8 to 10 minutes or until cheese is bubbly.

Source: Nicole Chambers

GINGER SALMON

This dish was included for those who love fish! The high calorie count is offset by its otherwise great nutritional value. Pair with Asian Cucumber Salad to balance calories.

4 servings

Ginger Salmon recipe
⅓ cup **ginger root, fresh, minced**
4 medium **green onions, sliced thin**
4 cloves **garlic, minced**
¼ cup **peanut oil**
2 tablespoons **peanut oil**
1 lb. **salmon fillets**
sea salt
black pepper, ground
2 tablespoons **honey**

NUTRITION FACTS	
Servings:	4
Amount Per Serving	
Calories:	461
Total Fat:	31.47 g
Cholesterol:	62 mg
Sodium:	70 mg
Total Carbs:	12.17 g
Dietary Fiber:	0.63 g
Sugars:	9.14 g
Protein:	23.80 g

1. Combine ginger, green onions, and garlic in a small bowl. Heat peanut oil in a small saucepan over high heat until very hot. Remove from heat, and stir in the ginger mixture; set aside.

68

2. Preheat oven to 425 F.

3. Heat 2T peanut oil in a large, ovenproof, nonstick skillet over medium-high heat. Season salmon to taste with salt and pepper. Sear salmon until golden brown on both sides, 30 to 40 seconds per side. Transfer to a plate, and wipe excess oil from skillet. Spread honey over top of fillets. Spread with ginger paste from step 1.

4. Place salmon into the skillet, and place in preheated oven. Bake for 10 minutes, or until salmon is cooked in center.

You may substitute 3/4 teaspoon powdered ginger for the fresh ginger root but the result will be less 'zippy'.

Source: adapted from Ryan Nomura's Ginger-Scallion Crusted Salmon

SHRIMP AND TOMATO LINGUINI

4 servings

Shrimp and Tomato Linguini recipe
1 lb. **linguini**
1 tablespoon **olive oil**
1 ½ tablespoons **olive oil**
¼ cup **onion, chopped**
1 tablespoon **garlic**
½ teaspoon **basil, dried**
salt and pepper to taste
¼ cup **cooking sherry**
1 cup **tomatoes, stewed**
          w/ **oregano & garlic**
½ lb. **shrimp, precooked**
½ cup **romano cheese, grated**

NUTRITION FACTS	
Servings:	4
Amount Per Serving	
Calories:	387
Total Fat:	29.47 g
Cholesterol:	176 mg
Sodium:	785 mg
Total Carbs:	49.13 g
Dietary Fiber:	2.54 g
Sugars:	4.01 g
Protein:	31.15 g

1. Bring a large pot of water to a boil. Add pasta and cook for 5 to 6 minutes or until al dente; drain. Mix in 1 T of the olive oil. Cover to keep warm.

2. Heat the 1 1/2 T of olive oil in a skillet over medium heat. Stir in onion, garlic and basil and cook until onion is tender. Season to taste with salt and pepper. Add wine and tomatoes. Continue to cook for 10 minutes, stirring occasionally.

3. Add shrimp to skillet, stirring until just heated. Pour over pasta and toss. Top with romano cheese and serve.

Source: Nicole Chambers

FACTOIDS

✦ *Weigh in before and after training to monitor fluid loss. Drink two cups of fluid for every pound of body weight lost.*

✦ *Meals are best eaten three to four hours before competition.*

✦ *A fluid loss of 23% can quickly occur during intense training.*

✦ *Fasting quickly reduces your blood sugar, which in turn robs your brain and muscles of their most important energy source.*

✦ *The greater the peaks and valleys in your body weight, the more difficult it is for your body to function correctly.*

✦ *Drink 8 oz. of fluid every 15 to 20 minutes during training and competition.*

✦ *Studies have shown that alternating between feast and famine may cause your body to metabolize more slowly. Yo-yo dieting just makes cutting weight more difficult.*

✦ *Limit your use of butter, margarine, mayonnaise, sour cream, cream cheese, and regular salad dressings. Instead, use barbeque sauce, ketchup, mustard, relish, and vegetables for toppings.*

✦ *Switching to skim milk can make a dramatic difference in caloric and fat intake.*

✦ *The darker the urine the more dehydrated you are.*

✦ *A baked potato has almost no fat, a minimal amount of sodium and a good supply of complex carbohydrates.*

✦ *Sports drinks that contain less than 5% carbohydrate do not provide enough energy to improve your performance.*

Chapter 7
Side Dishes

SEASONED BARLEY

4 servings

Seasoned Barley recipe
1 tablespoon **olive oil**
½ cup **mushrooms, fresh, sliced**
2 ¼ cups **water**
1 teaspoon **chicken bouillon**
⅛ teaspoon **sage, ground**
¼ teaspoon **rosemary, dried**
½ teaspoon **garlic powder**
2 tablespoons **cooking sherry**
1 cup **barley, rinsed**

NUTRITION FACTS	
Servings:	4
Amount Per Serving	
Calories:	214
Total Fat:	3.92 g
Cholesterol:	0 mg
Sodium:	288 mg
Total Carbs:	39.98 g
Dietary Fiber:	7.95 g
Sugars:	0.86 g
Protein:	5.47 g

1. In small frying pan, heat olive oil and saute mushrooms until limp. Do not drain. Set aside.

2. In medium saucepan, bring to boil water, bouillon, sage, rosemary, garlic, and sherry. Add barley and mushroom/olive oil saute'. Return to boil. Reduce heat and simmer for 20 minutes or until desired tenderness is achieved.

Source: Nicole Chambers

BROWN & WILD RICE

6 servings

Brown & Wild Rice recipe
2 tablespoons **butter**
½ lb. **mushrooms, sliced**
½ cup **onion, chopped**
2 cups **chicken broth, fat free**
½ cup **wild rice**
½ cup **brown rice**
2 tablespoons **butter**
1 teaspoon **sea salt**

NUTRITION FACTS	
Servings:	6
Amount Per Serving	
Calories:	194
Total Fat:	7.76 g
Cholesterol:	20 mg
Sodium:	768 mg
Total Carbs:	26.07 g
Dietary Fiber:	2.26 g
Sugars:	2.05 g
Protein:	5.06 g

1. Preheat oven to 350 degrees F.

2. Melt 2T butter in a medium skillet over medium heat. Place mushrooms and onion in skillet, cook until tender. Set aside.

3. In medium saucepan, bring chicken broth to a boil. Add wild rice, cover and simmer for 12 minutes. Return to boil and add brown rice. Reduce to simmer and cook covered for 45 minutes.

4. Transfer to 1-1/2 quart baking dish, add mushroom/onion saute', 2T butter and salt. Stir.

5. Cover, and bake in the preheated oven 30 minutes.

Source: Nicole Chambers

MEXICAN BROWN RICE

6 servings

Mexican Brown Rice recipe
1 cup **brown rice**
1 tablespoon **olive oil**
1 clove **garlic, halved**
½ cup **onion, finely chopped**
¼ cup **bell pepper, green, finely chopped**
¼ cup **jalapeno peppers, chopped**
¾ cup **tomatoes, canned, diced w/ juice, drained**
1 ½ cups **chicken broth, fat free**
1 teaspoon **chicken bouillon**
salt and pepper to taste
½ teaspoon **cumin, ground**
½ cup **cilantro, fresh**

NUTRITION FACTS	
Servings:	6
Amount Per Serving	
Calories:	151
Total Fat:	3.12 g
Cholesterol:	0 mg
Sodium:	394 mg
Total Carbs:	27.26 g
Dietary Fiber:	1.85 g
Sugars:	1.68 g
Protein:	3.32 g

1. In a medium sauce pan, saute rice in hot oil over medium heat for about 2 minutes. Add garlic, onion, peppers and tomato. Saute together for 1 minute. Pour in chicken broth, and bring to a boil. Season with bouillon, salt and pepper, cumin, and cilantro. Bring to a boil, cover, and reduce heat to low. Cook for 20 minutes. Remove from heat and let sit for 5 minutes.

Source: unknown

BROWN SUGAR BAKED BEANS

8 servings

Brown Sugar Baked Beans recipe

½ lb. **ground beef, 85% lean**

½ lb. **bacon, cooked, chopped**

1 cup **onion, chopped**

½ cup **brown sugar**

¼ cup **ketchup**

¼ cup **barbecue sauce**

1 tablespoon **mustard, prepared**

½ teaspoon **black pepper, ground**

½ teaspoon **chili powder**

1 ½ cups **pork and beans, canned, undrained**

1 ½ cups **kidney beans, canned, drained**

1 ½ cups **great northern beans, canned, drained**

NUTRITION FACTS	
Servings:	8
Amount Per Serving	
Calories:	441
Total Fat:	14.63 g
Cholesterol:	53 mg
Sodium:	1194 mg
Total Carbs:	47.59 g
Dietary Fiber:	8.15 g
Sugars:	22.14 g
Protein:	24.99 g

1. In a large skillet, cook beef and onion until meat is done and onion is tender. Drain.

2. Combine beef and onion mixture with all remaining ingredients except beans and mix well. Stir in beans. Cook on low for four hours in slow cooker.

Source: adapted from Kathy Schultz's Old Settlers' Baked Beans

QUINOA WITH BLACK BEANS AND CORN

4 servings

Quinoa with Black Beans and Corn recipe
1 teaspoon **olive oil**
½ medium **onion, chopped**
2 cloves **garlic, peeled and chopped**
⅜ cup **quinoa**
¾ cups **vegetable broth**
½ teaspoon **cumin, ground**
⅛ teaspoon **cayenne pepper**
salt and pepper to taste
½ cup **corn, canned, drained**
2 cups **black beans, canned drained**

NUTRITION FACTS	
Servings:	4
Amount Per Serving	
Calories:	207
Total Fat:	2.53 g
Cholesterol:	0 mg
Sodium:	382 mg
Total Carbs:	36.77 g
Dietary Fiber:	9.29 g
Sugars:	1.41 g
Protein:	10.69 g

1. Saute onion and garlic in olive oil until lightly browned.

2. Add quinoa and cook on medium low for 2 minutes. Add vegetable broth, cumin, cayenne pepper, salt, and pepper and bring to boil. Cover, reduce heat, and simmer 20 minutes,

3. Add corn and black beans. Simmer 5 minutes. Remove from heat. Let rest for 5 minutes. Toss gently and serve.

Source: Nicole Chambers

FACTOIDS

✦ *Foods like applesauce, crackers and cereal can be easily digested and aid in recovery.*

✦ *It is important to drink plenty of fluids during practice and between matches. Not only will you feel better, but you may also find you have more endurance.*

✦ *Chewing your food thoroughly stimulates enzyme secretion in the mouth & digestive tract for healthier digestion.*

✦ *Fasting slows metabolism.*

✦ *You can only lose 2-3 lbs. of fat per week…anything else is just water.*

✦ *A mere 2% drop in body water can trigger fuzzy short-term memory and trouble with basic math.*

✦ *Eat fiber in the morning to decrease your appetite all day.*

✦ *Six small meals a day is the healthiest way to lose and keep weight off.*

✦ *The object is to lose FAT-not water.*

✦ *8-ounce serving of a sports drink with 6% - 8% carbohydrates (sugars) and about 110 mg of sodium absorbs into your body faster than plain water and can provide energy to working muscles that water cannot.*

✦ *A big evening meal builds deposits of fat because of inactivity.*

✦ *Good fats include olive oil (unheated), avocados, peanuts, pistachios, Omega 3's (fish) and a moderate consumption of eggs.*

Chapter 8

Vegetables

SWEET DILL CARROTS

4 servings

Sweet Dill Carrots recipe
1 lb. **carrots, baby**
2 tablespoons **butter**
2 tablespoons **brown sugar**
½ teaspoon **dill, dried**
salt and pepper to taste

NUTRITION FACTS	
Servings:	4
Amount Per Serving	
Calories:	123
Total Fat:	5.55 g
Cholesterol:	15 mg
Sodium:	130 mg
Total Carbs:	17.78 g
Dietary Fiber:	3.19 g
Sugars:	12.22 g
Protein:	1.14 g

1. In microwave safe bowl, cover carrots and cook on high in microwave for 4 minutes. Drain.

2. Melt butter in medium saucepan. Add brown sugar, dill, salt, and pepper and stir until well combined. Add carrots and gently toss to cover. Serve hot.

Source: Nicole Chambers

BAKED ASPARAGUS

4 servings

Baked Asparagus recipe

1 bunch **asparagus, fresh
        trimmed**

1 tablespoon **olive oil**

1 dash **sea salt, to taste**

1 dash **black pepper, ground,
        to taste**

2 tablespoons **butter**

1 tablespoon **soy sauce, light**

2 tablespoons **balsamic vinegar**

NUTRITION FACTS	
Servings:	4
Amount Per Serving	
Calories:	69
Total Fat:	5.40 g
Cholesterol:	15 mg
Sodium:	222 mg
Total Carbs:	3.68 g
Dietary Fiber:	1.10 g
Sugars:	2.21 g
Protein:	1.42 g

1. Preheat oven to 350 degrees F.

2. Place asparagus, olive oil and salt and pepper in large bowl. Toss gently to coat.

3. Transfer to baking dish. Cover and bake asparagus for 10 to15 minutes in preheated oven, or until al dente.

4. Brown butter in small pan over medium heat. Stir in soy sauce and balsamic vinegar. Serve asparagus with butter sauce.

Source: Nicole Chambers

ROASTED BEETS WITH SAUTEED GREENS

4 servings

Roasted Beets with Sauteed Greens recipe
1 bunch **beets (4 to 5, med size)**
1 bunch **beet greens, cut**
          from bunch
2 tablespoon **olive oil**
1 tablespoon **butter**
2 tablespoons **olive oil**
2 cloves **garlic, minced**
2 tablespoons **onion**
1 tablespoon **red wine vinegar**
salt and pepper to taste

NUTRITION FACTS	
Servings:	4
Amount Per Serving	
Calories:	145
Total Fat:	13.20 g
Cholesterol:	0 mg
Sodium:	40 mg
Total Carbs:	5.85 g
Dietary Fiber:	1.54 g
Sugars:	3.67 g
Protein:	0.97 g

1. Preheat the oven to 350 F. Remove beet greens and scrub beets. Rinse greens, removing any large stems. Set aside. Place the beets in a small baking dish or roasting pan, and toss with 2 tablespoons of olive oil.

2. Cover, and bake for 45 to 60 minutes, or until a knife can slide easily through the largest beet.

3. Beets are easily peeled after they have been roasted, if you desire. Cut beets into cubes or slices and set aside.

4. Melt butter and 2T olive oil in a large skillet over medium-low heat, add garlic and onion and saute for 1 minute. Tear the beet greens into 2 to 3 inch pieces, and add to skillet. Add vinegar and cook until greens are wilted and tender, stirring often. Season with salt and pepper. Serve sliced beets atop sauteed greens.

Source: unknown

BROCCOLI WITH CASHEWS

6 servings

Broccoli with Cashews recipe

3 bunches **broccoli crowns, cut from stems**

6 tablespoons **butter**

1 tablespoon **honey**

3 tablespoons **soy sauce, light**

2 teaspoons **cider vinegar**

2 cloves **garlic, minced**

¼ teaspoon **black pepper, ground**

⅓ cup **cashews, chopped**

NUTRITION FACTS	
Servings:	6
Amount Per Serving	
Calories:	303
Total Fat:	13.30 g
Cholesterol:	27 mg
Sodium:	508 mg
Total Carbs:	36.14 g
Dietary Fiber:	12.19 g
Sugars:	10.58 g
Protein:	14.62 g

1. Cover broccoli and cook in microwave on high for 3 minutes. Drain.

2. Melt butter in a saucepan over medium heat. Add honey, soy sauce, vinegar, garlic, pepper and cashews. Bring just to boil and remove from heat.

3. Toss broccoli and sauce together. Serve hot.

Source: Nicole Chambers

COLLARD GREENS

The bacon fat gives this recipe its flavor. Pair with a low fat main dish for balance.

6 servings

Collard Greens recipe
1 tablespoon **olive oil**
10 slices **bacon, raw**
1 large **onion, chopped**
2 cloves **garlic powder, chopped**
1 lb. **collard greens, fresh, cut into 2" pieces**
3 cups **chicken broth, fat free**
1 tablespoon **apple cider vinegar**
2 teaspoons **brown sugar**
1 teaspoon **sea salt**
½ teaspoon **black pepper, ground**
2 dashes **cayenne pepper**

NUTRITION FACTS	
Servings:	6
Amount Per Serving	
Calories:	137
Total Fat:	7.15 g
Cholesterol:	14 mg
Sodium:	1188 mg
Total Carbs:	9.55 g
Dietary Fiber:	3.35 g
Sugars:	3.14 g
Protein:	8.00 g

1. Heat oil in a large pot over medium-high heat. Add bacon, and cook until crisp. Remove bacon from pan, crumble and return to the pan. Add onion, and cook until tender, about 5 minutes. Add garlic, and cook until just fragrant. Add collard greens, and fry until they start to wilt.

2. Pour in chicken broth and vinegar. Add brown sugar, salt, pepper, and cayenne pepper. Reduce heat to low, cover, and simmer for 1 hour.

Source: adapted from Ken Adam's Kickin Collard Greens

WHITE CORN & ROASTED RED PEPPERS

This tasty side dish is somewhat high in calories. Pair with a low calorie main dish so it will average out.

8 servings

White Corn & Roasted Red Pepper recipe

6 tablespoons **butter**

1 teaspoon **seasoned salt**

¾ teaspoon **black pepper, ground**

¼ cup **zucchini, diced**

4 cups **corn, white, frozen, thawed and drained**

6 oz. **red peppers, roasted, chopped**

NUTRITION FACTS	
Servings:	8
Amount Per Serving	
Calories:	194
Total Fat:	11.21 g
Cholesterol:	0 mg
Sodium:	308 mg
Total Carbs:	21.67 g
Dietary Fiber:	2.04 g
Sugars:	7.40 g
Protein:	2.50 g

1. Melt butter in large saucepan. Stir in salt and pepper. Add diced zucchini and saute for 2 minutes.

2. Add corn and roasted peppers to butter mixture. Stir gently and cook uncovered over medium low heat for 3 minutes. Serve hot.

Source: Nicole Chambers

COUNTRY GREEN BEANS

4 servings

Country Green Beans recipe
1 lb. **green beans, trimmed**
¼ cup **onion, chopped**
¼ cup **butter**
¼ cup **chicken broth, fat free**
1 teaspoon **garlic powder**
½ teaspoon **sea salt**
¼ teaspoon **black pepper, ground**
4 slices **bacon, cooked, crumbled**

NUTRITION FACTS	
Servings:	4
Amount Per Serving	
Calories:	185
Total Fat:	13.74 g
Cholesterol:	39 mg
Sodium:	648 mg
Total Carbs:	9.64 g
Dietary Fiber:	3.34 g
Sugars:	4.17 g
Protein:	5.55 g

1. In a saucepan, combine all ingredients EXCEPT bacon. Cover and simmer for 15–20 minutes or until beans are tender.

2. Remove from heat. Add bacon and toss.

Source: Nicole Chambers

85

GREEN BEANS AND CARROTS

6 servings

Green Bean and Carrot recipe

1 lb. **green beans, cut into 1" lengths**

2 medium **carrots, cut into 1/2" strips**

4 tablespoons **butter**

4 tablespoons **olive oil**

¼ teaspoon **garlic powder**

1 medium **onion, sliced**

½ lb. **mushrooms, fresh, sliced**

1 teaspoon **seasoned salt**

¼ teaspoon **black pepper, ground**

NUTRITION FACTS	
Servings:	6
Amount Per Serving	
Calories:	204
Total Fat:	16.21 g
Cholesterol:	20 mg
Sodium:	102 mg
Total Carbs:	12.44 g
Dietary Fiber:	3.94 g
Sugars:	5.93 g
Protein:	3.27 g

1. Parboil green beans and carrots for 3 minutes. Drain and set aside.

2. Add butter, olive oil and garlic powder to large skillet and cook over medium heat. Add onions and mushrooms. Saute' until almost tender. Reduce heat, cover, and simmer 3 minutes.

3. Add green beans, carrots, seasoned salt and pepper to onion mixture. Toss gently to coat. Cook on low for 5 minutes.

Source: Nicole Chambers

BAKED TURNIPS

4 servings

Baked Turnips recipe
3 cups **turnip, peeled, 1/2" slices**
3 tablespoons **butter, softned**
1 can **ginger ale, enough
    to cover**
1 pinch **marjoram, dried**
salt and pepper to taste

NUTRITION FACTS	
Servings:	4
Amount Per Serving	
Calories:	140
Total Fat:	8.10 g
Cholesterol:	22 mg
Sodium:	140 mg
Total Carbs:	9.06 g
Dietary Fiber:	1.65 g
Sugars:	3.48 g
Protein:	1.33 g

1. Preheat an oven to 350 degrees F.

2. Parboil turnips in large pot for approximately 5 to 7 minutes. Drain.

3. Gently toss turnips in large bowl with butter, ginger ale, marjoram, salt and pepper.

4. Transfer mixture to baking dish and bake uncovered for 1 hour.

Source: Nicole Chambers

KALE AND SPINACH WITH CASHEWS

4 servings

Kale and Spinach with cashews recipe
½ cup **cashews**
1 tablespoon **olive oil**
1 tablespoons **butter**
2 tablespoons **olive oil**
1 medium **onion, minced**
5 cloves **garlic, minced**
1 lb. **kale, stems removed**
1 bag **spinach, fresh**
1 dash **sea salt**
1 dash **black pepper, ground**

NUTRITION FACTS	
Servings:	4
Amount Per Serving	
Calories:	305
Total Fat:	20.90 g
Cholesterol:	7 mg
Sodium:	181 mg
Total Carbs:	23.87 g
Dietary Fiber:	5.21 g
Sugars:	2.42 g
Protein:	9.37 g

1. Preheat oven to 350 degrees F.

2. Combine the cashews and 1 tablespoon olive oil in a bowl; toss to coat the cashews in the oil. Spread onto a baking sheet.

3. Toast the cashews in the preheated oven for about 5 to 10 minutes, until golden brown, shaking the baking sheet occasionally. Set aside.

4. Heat butter and olive oil in a large skillet over medium heat. Cook and stir the onion in the hot oil until the onion softens, about 5 minutes. Add garlic and cook for 1 minute. Add kale to the onion and garlic mixture and stir until kale starts to wilt. Reduce heat to medium low, cover and cook, stirring occasionally, until the kale softens, about 7 minutes. Stir the spinach into the mixture, season with the sea salt and pepper, and continue cooking until the spinach wilts, about 3 minutes. Mix in cashews and serve.

Source: adapted from Dawn's Kale Side dish, Allrecipes

SWEET POTATO CASSEROLE

8 servings

Sweet Potato Casserole recipe
cooking spray
5 medium **sweet potatoes**
¼ teaspoon **sea salt**
¼ cup **butter**
2 medium **eggs**
1 teaspoon **vanilla extract**
½ teaspoon **cinnamon, ground**
⅓ cup **natural sugar**
2 tablespoons **light cream**
¼ cup **butter**
3 tablespoons **all-purpose flour**
⅔ cup **brown sugar**
½ cup **pecans, chopped**

NUTRITION FACTS	
Servings:	8
Amount Per Serving	
Calories:	357
Total Fat:	17.13 g
Cholesterol:	73 mg
Sodium:	222 mg
Total Carbs:	46.82 g
Dietary Fiber:	3.18 g
Sugars:	32.27 g
Protein:	3.83 g

1. Preheat oven to 350 degrees F. Spray a 9x13 inch baking dish with cooking spray.

2. Peel sweet potatoes. Cut into 1" slices and boil until fork tender. Drain and mash.

3. In a large bowl, whip the mashed sweet potatoes, salt, 1/4 cup butter, eggs, vanilla extract, cinnamon, sugar, and light cream together until well blended. Transfer to the prepared baking dish.

4. In a medium bowl, combine 1/4 cup butter, flour, brown sugar, and chopped pecans. Mix with a pastry blender or your fingers to the consistency of course meal. Sprinkle over the sweet potato mixture.

5. Bake in preheated oven for 30 minutes or until topping is crisp and lightly browned.

Source: adapted from Heather's Gourmet Sweet Potato Classic

ZUCCHINI JAPANESE STYLE

4 servings

Zucchini Japanese Style recipe

2 tablespoons **sesame oil**

1 medium **onion, thinly sliced**

2 medium **zucchini, cut into
thin strips**

2 tablespoons **teriyaki sauce,
low salt**

1 tablespoon **soy sauce, light**

1 tablespoon **sesame seeds, white**

1 dash **black pepper, ground**

NUTRITION FACTS	
Servings:	4
Amount Per Serving	
Calories:	108
Total Fat:	7.79 g
Cholesterol:	0 mg
Sodium:	268 mg
Total Carbs:	7.59 g
Dietary Fiber:	1.75 g
Sugars:	4.69 g
Protein:	2.52 g

1. In large frying pan, saute onions in sesame oil over medium heat for 5 minutes. Raise heat to medium high and add zucchini. Cook for 1 minute, stirring often.

2. Lower heat to medium. Stir in teriyaki, soy, sesame seeds and pepper. Continue cooking on low for 5 minutes. Serve hot.

Source: adapted from Michelle B's Japanese Zucchini and Onions

92

FACTOIDS

✦ *Eating slowly will help speed sense of fullness.*

✦ *One glass of water can shut down midnight hunger pangs.*

✦ *Proteins such as chicken, red meat, nuts and beans are vital for high school wrestlers because they provide muscles with the amino acids necessary to recover from vigorous exercise.*

✦ *Dieting & intense workouts lower the immune system.*

✦ *Grains, lentils and brown rice are a few foods packed with complex carbs.*

✦ *Drink 16 oz. of fluid 2 hours before training or competition.*

✦ *Eat 60 to 65 grams of fat daily and avoid saturated fats.*

✦ *Egg whites and tuna are low-fat options that also have muscle-supporting qualities.*

✦ *It is advisable to eat foods high in antioxidants, which help the body fend off infection.*

✦ *Lack of water is the #1 trigger of daytime fatigue.*

✦ *Some examples of foods and spices high in antioxidants include berries, oranges, plums, nuts, seeds, ginger and oregano.*

✦ *Low energy intake and dehydration hurt muscular endurance and lead to stale performance on the mat.*

✦ *Pack high-carbohydrate snacks for tournaments: low-fat granola bars, pretzels, bagels, crackers, high-carbohydrate energy bars, fig bars and fruit.*

Chapter 9

Desserts

CRANBERRY CARROT CAKE

12 servings

Cranberry Carrot Cake recipe
2 cups **flour**
2 teaspoons **baking soda**
1 tablespoon **baking powder**
2 teaspoons **cinnamon, ground**
½ teaspoon **ginger powder**
1 pinch **sea salt**
1 ½ cups **natural sugar**
1 cup **mayonnaise, light**
3 medium **eggs**
2 teaspoons **vanilla extract**
2 cups **carrots, shredded**
1 cup **pineapple, crushed, natural juices, with juice**
4 oz. **pecans, chopped**
¾ cup **cranberries, dried**

NUTRITION FACTS	
Servings:	12
Amount Per Serving	
Calories:	345
Total Fat:	11.27 g
Cholesterol:	45 mg
Sodium:	405 mg
Total Carbs:	56.83 g
Dietary Fiber:	2.76 g
Sugars:	34.65 g
Protein:	4.6 g

1. Preheat oven to 350 degrees F. Grease and flour 3 – 8" round cake pans. In medium bowl, whisk together flour, baking soda, baking powder, cinnamon, ginger, and salt. Set aside.

2. Cream sugar, mayonnaise, eggs, and vanilla extract with an electric mixer until blended, scraping the bowl occasionally. Stir in the flour mixture, then fold in the carrots, pineapple, pecans, and cranberries. Divide evenly between the prepared cake pans.

3. Bake in preheated oven until a toothpick inserted into the center comes out clean, 30 to 35 minutes. Cool in the pan for 10 minutes, then remove from the pan, and allow to cool completely on a wire rack.

4. Eat plain or frost with your favorite cream cheese frosting.

Source: adapted from Jo Wolf's Cranberry Carrot Cake

GRANOLA BARS

Nutritional calculation includes chocolate chips.

24 servings

Granola Bars recipe
2 ½ cups **cereal, crispy rice**
2 cups **oats, quick cooking**
⅓ cup **raisins**
⅓ cup **cranberries, dried**
½ cup **pecans, chopped**
⅓ cup **sunflower seeds**
⅓ cup **chocolate chips, mini**
½ cup **brown sugar**
⅔ cup **honey**
⅜ teaspoon **sea salt**
1 cup **peanut butter, crunchy**
1 teaspoon **vanilla extract**

NUTRITION FACTS	
Servings:	24
Amount Per Serving	
Calories:	151
Total Fat:	4.23 g
Cholesterol:	0 mg
Sodium:	54 mg
Total Carbs:	26.79 g
Dietary Fiber:	2.09 g
Sugars:	17.37 g
Protein:	4.33 g

1. Grease a 9x13 inch baking dish with cooking spray. In a large bowl, stir together the rice cereal, oats, raisins, cranberries, pecans and sunflower seeds and set aside.

2. Combine brown sugar and honey in a small saucepan over medium heat. Heat just until boiling, then remove from heat and stir in sea salt, peanut butter and vanilla until smooth. Pour over the cereal and oat mixture, and mix well.

3. Transfer mix into the prepared pan. Add chocolate chips and press mix into the pan until very dense. Allow to cool, and cut into bars.

note: *for crispier bars, cook in 100 degree oven for 90 minutes; cut with serrated knife before fully cooled*

Source: adapted from Tina Maries' Gobble Up Granola Snacks

HOMEMADE APPLESAUCE

You can make this in the slow cooker by combining all ingredients and setting on low for 6 – 8 hrs. Mash after cooking.

6 servings

Homemade Applesauce recipe

6 medium **apples, cored and chopped**

1 cup **water**

2 tablespoons **natural sugar**

1 dash **allspice**

⅛ teaspoon **cinnamon, ground**

NUTRITION FACTS	
Servings:	6
Amount Per Serving	
Calories:	93
Total Fat:	.10 g
Cholesterol:	0 mg
Sodium:	0 mg
Total Carbs:	24.78 g
Dietary Fiber:	2.12 g
Sugars:	20.43 g
Protein:	0.44 g

In a saucepan, combine apples, water, sugar, allspice and cinnamon. Cover, and cook over medium heat for 15 to 20 minutes, or until apples are soft. Once cool, mash with potato masher.

Source: Nicole Chambers

MANGO SORBET

6 servings

Mango Sorbet recipe

½ cup **water**

½ cup **natural sugar**

4 tablespoons **lime juice, fresh or bottled**

4 medium **mangoes, very ripe, peeled and cubed**

NUTRITION FACTS	
Servings:	6
Amount Per Serving	
Calories:	202
Total Fat:	0.69 g
Cholesterol:	0 mg
Sodium:	4 mg
Total Carbs:	50.87 g
Dietary Fiber:	3.62 g
Sugars:	47.27 g
Protein:	1.86 g

1. Bring the water to a boil. Dissolve the sugar into the boiling water, stirring constantly. Once the sugar is dissolved completely, remove the pan from the heat. (Note: Do not allow the syrup to boil for too long or the syrup will be too thick.)

2. Add lime juice to syrup and stir until well mixed. Set aside to cool and thicken.

3. Place cubed mango in a food processor, and puree. Pour in simple syrup and lime juice, and puree until smooth.

4. (Follow the directions in step 5 if you don't have an ice cream maker)
Place in an ice cream maker. Freeze thoroughly.

5. Chill in refrigerator for 2 hours. Transfer to freezer for 30 minutes. Remove from freezer and beat the mixture until creamy. Return to freezer for 30 minutes. Remove from freezer and beat with whisk. Repeat procedure 3 times, each time freezing for 30 minutes in between.

Source: Allrecipes, MarylandGirl's Mango Sorbet

Chapter 10

Drinks

HOMEMADE SPORTS DRINK

This one will save you a lot of money plus you choose the Kool–Aid flavor!

8 servings

Sports Drink recipe

7 cups **water**

1 packet **Kool–Aid packet, unsweetened**

¼ teaspoon **lite salt**

¼ teaspoon **sea salt**

½ cup **natural sugar**

NUTRITION FACTS	
Servings:	8
Amount Per Serving	
Calories:	49
Total Fat:	0 g
Cholesterol:	0 mg
Sodium:	145 mg
Total Carbs:	12.48 g
Dietary Fiber:	0 g
Sugars:	12.40 g
Protein:	0 g

Combine all ingredients in 64 oz container (an old juice jar works great). Shake until dissolved. Serve chilled.

Source: unknown

LOWFAT CHOCOLATE MILK

Very tasty while giving needed calcium.

1 servings

Lowfat Chocolate Milk recipe
4 oz. **milk, 99% fat free, warmed**
1 tablespoon **cocoa powder**
1 tablespoon **natural sugar**
8 oz. **milk, 99% fat free**

NUTRITION FACTS	
Servings:	1
Amount Per Serving	
Calories:	303
Total Fat:	4.28 g
Cholesterol:	16 mg
Sodium:	289 mg
Total Carbs:	52.99 g
Dietary Fiber:	1.04 g
Sugars:	48.54 g
Protein:	13.33 g

Mix warm milk, cocoa and sugar until dissolved. Chill if necessary. Add remaining milk. Stir and serve.

Source: Nicole Chambers

STRAWBERRY BANANA FRUIT SMOOTHIE

Everyone loves this one, and it's low in calories!

2 servings

Strawberry Banana Fruit Smoothie recipe

1 cup **V-8 splash peach mango drink**

1 cup **ice, crushed**

¼ cup **strawberries, frozen, thawed w/ juice**

½ **banana**

4 oz. **vanilla yogurt, lowfat**

NUTRITION FACTS	
Servings:	2
Amount Per Serving	
Calories:	164
Total Fat:	0.76 g
Cholesterol:	2 mg
Sodium:	71 mg
Total Carbs:	36.82 g
Dietary Fiber:	1.37 g
Sugars:	32.09 g
Protein:	3.79 g

In blender, combine juice and crushed ice. Blend until slurry is formed. Add strawberries and blend until just mixed. Add banana in several pieces and yogurt. Blend until smooth. Add more crushed ice if necessary.

Source: Nicole Chambers

VITAMIN C LEMONADE

An 8 oz glass of this lemonade tastes really good and also provides 2000mg of needed vitamin C to help the immune system. Vitamin C powder available online.

8 servings

Vitamin C Lemonade recipe

7 cups **water**

5 teaspoons **vitamin c powder (ascorbic acid)**

3/4 cup **sugar, white**

2 tablespoons **lemon juice**

NUTRITION FACTS	
Servings:	8
Amount Per Serving	
Calories:	74
Total Fat:	0.01 g
Cholesterol:	0 mg
Sodium:	0 mg
Total Carbs:	18.74 g
Dietary Fiber:	0.01 g
Sugars:	18.57 g
Protein:	0.01 g

Add water, vitamin c powder, sugar and lemon juice to a 64 oz container. Shake until dissolved. Pour over ice.

Source: Nicole Chambers

FACTOIDS

◆ *Dehydration is a major cause of reduction in strength and endurance.*

◆ *The wrong diet can leave a wrestler feeling weak, dehydrated, and cramped up.*

◆ *Successful wrestlers know that good nutrition is an essential component of their daily training ritual.*

◆ *Good eating habits help wrestlers compete at a much higher level.*

◆ *Avoid beverages containing alcohol and caffeine, as they promote dehydration.*

◆ *Eat smaller portions. Your metabolism speeds up and more calories are burned off.*

◆ *Gradual weight loss is best accomplished by combining your training with a slight reduction in food intake.*

◆ *Protein is not stored in the body, you must consume it daily.*

◆ *An 8 oz sports drink with 6% - 8% carbohydrates (sugars) and about 110 mg of sodium absorbs into your body faster than plain water and can provide energy to working muscles that water cannot.*

◆ *Maintain a fuller feeling for a longer duration by having a diet high in protein.*

◆ *It takes 3500 calories to burn 1 pound of fat.*

◆ *You need to eat (keep metabolism going) to lose weight. Eat every 4 hours.*

◆ *Wrestlers need to drink a minimum of 80-96 oz of fluids per day.*

Index

cinnamon, 8, 9, 10, 20, 24,
       26, 90, 94, 97
cocoa powder, 102
cola beverage, 55
collard greens recipe, 83
collard greens, 83
cooking sherry, 32, 64, 70, 72
coriander, ground, 62
corn meal, 18
corn, 62, 76
corn, frozen, 36, 40, 84
cornstarch, 34
cornucopia salad, 44
country green beans, 85
cranberries, dried, 8, 42, 44,
       45, 94
cranberry carrot cake, 94
cream of chicken soup, 60
cream of mushroom soup, 55
crushed red pepper, 34
cucumbers, 38
cumin, 30, 36, 40, 62, 74, 76
dill, dried, 38, 78
dressing, vinegrette, 45
eggs, 10, 11, 13, 14, 18, 20,
       22, 24, 26, 54, 90, 94
factoids, 7, 71, 77, 93, 105
flax seed, 14
flour, 66, 94
fruity romaine salad, 45
ginger ale, 87
ginger powder, 30, 34, 94
ginger root, fresh, 68
ginger salmon recipe, 68
granola bars, 96
grapes, 39
great northern beans, 75
green beans and carrots, 86
green beans, 85, 86
green onions, 44, 68
grilled pork tenderloin in
   greek marinade, 48

ground beef, 52, 54, 75
ham steak, cooked, 32
healthy grain bread, 14
hearty oatmeal, 8
homemade applesauce, 97
honey, 10, 14, 16, 16, 18,
       58, 66, 68, 82, 96
hot pepper sauce, 40, 52
jalapeno peppers, 74
kale, 88
kale & spinach w/cashews, 88
ketchup, 54, 75
kidney beans, 40, 75
kool-aid, 101
lamb & barley soup, 29
lamb stew, 64
lamb, stew meat, 29, 64
lemon chicken w/ pasta, 59
lemon herb pork chops, 49
lemon juice, 14, 40, 49, 59,
lettuce, red leaf, 44
lettuce, romaine, 45
light cream, 90
lime juice, 40, 48, 98
linguini, 70
lowfat asian style soup, 34
lowfat chocolate milk, 102
mandarin oranges, 42, 45
mango sorbet, 98
mangoes, 98
marjoram, dried, 32, 87
mayonnaise, light, 39, 94
mexican brown rice, 74
milk, fat free, 9, 10, 11, 13
       22, 26, 102, 102
milk, dry powder, non-fat, 18
mirin (japanese rice wine), 38
molasses, 14
morning glory muffins, 24
mozzarella, non-fat, 66
mushrooms, 34, 50, 72, 86
mustard, prepared, 75

no-knead wheat rolls, 13
nutmeg, 10
oats, 8, 22, 96
onion soup mix, 54, 64
onion, red, 39, 62
onion, sweet, 32, 52, 64
orange juice, 10
oregano, 48, 52, 56, 62
peanut butter, 96
peanut oil, 68, 68
pear, 45
pecans, 8, 42, 90, 94, 96
perfect spinach salad, 42
pine nuts, 42
pineapple, crushed, 94
pinto beans, 36
pork and beans, 75
pork loin chops, 49
pork roast, boston butt, 47
pork tenderloin, 48, 50
pot roast recipe, 55
potatoes, 32, 64
quinoa, 9, 76
quinoa black beans & corn, 76
raisins, 8, 24, 96
really tender pork roast, 47
red lentils, 30
red peppers, roasted, 84
red wine, 50
red wine vinegar, 40, 44, 80
rempel family meatloaf, 54
rice wine vinegar, 34, 38
roasted beets with greens, 80
romano cheese, 70
rosemary, 29, 57, 59, 72
sage, ground, 32, 72
salmon filets, 68
salsa verde, 62
sesame oil, 38 ,92
sesame seeds, 38, 42, 92
shrimp & tomato linguini, 70
shrimp, 34, 70
sirloin tip roast, 56

sour cream, 52, 60
soy sauce, 34, 79, 82, 92
spanish chicken and rice, 60
spinach, 34, 42, 88
split pea and ham soup, 32
sports drink recipe, 101
steak sauce, 54, 58
strawberries, frozen, 103
strawberry banana smoothie, 103
sunflower seeds, 14, 39
sweet dill carrots, 78
sweet potato casserole, 90
sweet potato, carrot, apple, &
    red lentil soup, 30
sweet potato, 30, 90
swiss cheese, lowfat, 45
teriyaki sauce, 92
three bean salad, 40
thyme, 29, 56, 57, 59, 64
tomato paste, 52
tomato sauce, 36, 66
tomatoes, diced, 52, 57, 62, 74
tomatoes, stewed, 29, 36, 70
tortilla chicken & veg soup, 36
tortilla chips, 36, 62
turnip, 87
v-8 splash peach mango, 103
vanilla yogurt, 103
vitamin c lemonade, 104
walnuts, 9, 20, 22, 24
wheat bran, 14 26
white beans, 62
white corn & roasted red
    pepper, 84
white wine, 50
whole wheat blueberry pancake, 11
whole wheat bread recipe, 16
whole wheat pizza, 66
wild rice, 73
worcestershire sauce, 52, 58
zucchini, 20, 84, 92
zucchini bread, 20
zucchini japanese style, 92

Many thanks to the following sources. Their articles provided the basis for the "Factoid" information found throughout The Wrestler's Cookbook.

Sources of Reference:

California Interscholastic Federation 2011, 'Wrestlers' Diet – A Healthy Guide to Weight Control',cifstate.org, 26 August, <http://www.cifstate.org/index.php/component/content/article/81-resources/424-wrestlers-diet->

Herman, Jeff 2011, 'Diet for High School Wrestlers', livestrong.com, 14 June, <http://www.livestrong.com/article/293520-diet-for-high-school-wrestlers/>

Kimpel, Steve 2003, 'Feeding The Tiger Cubs – A strategy for energy intake during competition for young wrestlers', online PDF, 19 May, <www.leaguelineup.com/clwizards/files/FeedingTheTigerCubs.pdf>

Swertfager, Bill 2011, 'Wrestling Weight Control System – 38 Diet Tips & Facts for Wrestlers', sectiononewrestling.com, 15 April, <http://www.sectiononewrestling.com/documents/wrestling_weight_control_diet_facts.html>

USA Wrestling, CT 2009, 'Wrestlers Diet', <http://usawct.org/coachescorner/diet.php>

Yacono, Don 2008, 'The Wrestler's Diet', ezinearticles.com, 15 October, <http://ezinearticles.com/?The-Wrestlers-Diet&id=1570141>

56796432R00071

Made in the USA
San Bernardino, CA
14 November 2017